Contents

Foreword

Anyone reading this book before applying to medical school should give themselves a pat on the back: it takes courage and commitment to embark on a career in medicine. The choice you are making is a big one, but one that few regret. The medical school experience is unlike any other degree, and over the duration of the course you will develop a wealth of scientific and practical knowledge, applying it to positively influence the lives of the patients you encounter. It is a unique education: one that is to be valued and respected.

Just as a career as a doctor is different to most other careers, so too is the process of application to medical school. Universities are not simply trying to select the most academically able students. Instead, they aim to identify those who will make excellent doctors in the future. This means that the process of applying to medical school is often more demanding than other courses.

While you are working hard to get the academic grades for a place at medical school, you must also make time to prepare for admissions tests and interviews. This can be a stressful time for students and their families. Throughout, it's important to remember that each stage of the application process is not an enemy to be fought, but rather an opportunity to show your potential as a future doctor. No one is trying to trip you up!

Across the country, medical schools differ in how they go about training students to become doctors. Some courses are very practical from the very start, while others hold back from interaction with patients and initially prioritise learning through lectures. You may be more suited to one course than another, and therefore interview panels may ask you to demonstrate your understanding of their course structure or teaching style. This isn't just to check that you've done your homework: they are trying to ensure they offer places to students who will thrive on their course, for their benefit and for yours.

The assessments that are a necessary part of most medical school applications aim to measure your understanding of the scientific principles underlying medicine, and also increasingly test a range of skills in situational judgement and critical thinking. While these tests may initially seem daunting, you will already have encountered most of the knowledge tested in your studies at school. Critical thinking and situational judgement may be less familiar and often require more preparation. These same testing methodologies are used well into your career as a doctor, and therefore preparation at this stage will not only help your application to medical school, but will also benefit you in your future career.

Unlike many university courses, most medical schools interview their applicants. As medicine is such a people-centred discipline, it is vital for medical schools to see beyond a student's academic results and appreciate the candidate as a future doctor. While interviews may at times have an academic focus, they mainly aim to give interviewers an idea of how suited you are to a career in medicine, and how well the university can work with you on your journey to becoming a doctor. For the most part, there are no right or wrong answers to these interview questions. Interviewers are looking for an insight into who you are as a person, your motivations for pursuing a career in medicine, and your understanding of what that will involve. They are looking to find intelligent, motivated, compassionate students who they can help grow into excellent doctors.

So what can you do to prepare for the application process? The first thing to do – and perhaps the most important – is to honestly assess whether a career in medicine is right for you. It is vital that you have an understanding of what it is like to be a doctor, and whether that connects with who you are and what you want to achieve. If you can, try to undertake work experience, or talk to people who work in healthcare. Try to volunteer with an organisation that provides help to others. It's for a very good reason that universities like to see you've undertaken some sort of experience like this.

Consulting those with experience of the medical school application process will prepare you for each opportunity you encounter, and help you to give the best possible impression of yourself as a future doctor. Dukes Medical Applications and the authors of this book are aiming to do exactly that. They offer a range of skills and expertise at every stage of the application process – from deciding which school to apply to, right through to the final interview. They don't aim to spoon-feed you the 'right' answers, but instead provide you with the skills and confidence to authentically demonstrate your potential as a doctor of the future.

Good luck as you embark on this exciting journey towards a truly rewarding and life-changing profession.

Dr Jonathan M. Clarke MA(Cantab) MB BChir MRCS MPH
Clinical Research Fellow, Centre for Health Policy,
Imperial College London Affiliate Member, Ariadne Labs,
Harvard TH Chan School of Public Health

Introduction

An offer to study medicine is the start of a long, challenging, and fascinating experience. Universities are looking not only for successful students, but future doctors. The different elements of the admissions process are put in place to find applicants who not only have the intellectual ability to succeed in medicine, but the motivation, stamina, and tenacity to excel.

The purpose of this book is to help you every step of the way, from the original decision on whether medicine is the right course for you, through to the application process and beyond to your future as a doctor. Each chapter will provide more in-depth information on different aspects of making an application, including choosing a university, sitting an admissions test, and receiving an interview. There is also specific advice for international students and students who have already received an undergraduate degree, as the requirements for these applicants vary.

DO I NEED TO COME FROM A CERTAIN BACKGROUND TO STUDY MEDICINE?

The answer to this question is most definitely no. From being a neurosurgeon to being a general practitioner, the variety of different careers in medicine requires people with different life experiences and from different backgrounds. To be able to ensure your patient feels safe, cared for and respected, and to be an excellent doctor, does not require a certain education, age, or family history of medical careers.

Whether you attend a state or an independent school, the admission tutors will be looking for the same criteria: your grades, academic potential, motivation and dedication to medicine. The best applicants will receive the places regardless of background.

DO I HAVE TO FIT AN ACADEMIC MOULD?

Yes and no. Medicine is not only a difficult course to be accepted on to, but it is also a very intellectually challenging course to study. As a result, tutors will be looking for the brightest students and the majority of people who apply will have exceptional grades. A good academic profile alone, however, is not a guarantee to being accepted to study medicine. Universities will also look at how you have proved your desire to study medicine through extracurricular work. In addition, they will be looking for any other skills you will bring to the university.

One way to stand out from the crowd is to explore your personal interests in medicine. This could be something you learned during your work experience, or something you have explored through reading. Being able to discuss a topic from a scientific point of view is a useful skill, but to make yourself stand out from other applicants, remember to discuss how the doctor treated the patient, the communication skills they showed, the rapport they built up with the family, and the way they worked as part of a multidisciplinary team. Anyone can learn about diseases and treatments but a great doctor is able to explain them clearly to everyone, listen and understand concerns, and to work as a team knowing when they need to ask for help themselves.

DO I NEED TO HAVE A CERTAIN PERSONALITY?

To succeed in medicine, you have to have the confidence to believe that you deserve a place to study and become successful. Whether you are quiet and reserved or loud and outgoing, the crucial element for success is being able to show your ability and potential to study medicine by engaging creatively and confidently with new topics.

Shyness and nerves are expected in interview environments, and the interviewer will not judge you on this. They will be looking to get to know you and your individual personality in order to assess whether they believe you would be the right fit for the course and the university. There is no perfect applicant or perfect personality for medicine - different personalities are what make excellent doctors in different fields.

This book has been compiled by numerous experts with personal experience of applying and working in medicine. Each chapter will educate you on the different stages of applying to study medicine to help you make informed decisions about your application. However, the book is only an aid to helping you become successful - medicine is a field that is constantly evolving and requires you to be proactive and take responsibility for your own learning and actions. Applying this attitude to your application and ensuring you work to the best of your ability is valuable for any course, but will particularly aid you in your future career as a doctor.

Dr Emma Brierley MB BChir MA(Hons) Cantab

Is Becoming a Doctor Right for Me?

by Dr Emma Brierley

Before choosing to apply for a Medicine degree, you need to be one hundred per cent certain that this is not only the course you want to study but also the career you wish to pursue. Becoming a doctor goes beyond five or six years at university. It is a commitment to a lifetime of learning, life-changing moments and extremely hard work. To apply for Medicine just because you have excellent grades, want a prestigious career, or have a family member who is a medic may lead to severe shock and disappointment when the realities of medicine kick in.

Making an important decision that will affect the rest of your life needs considerable thought. This chapter will discuss the advantages and disadvantages of medicine and help you to decide whether this is the journey you wish to begin.

ADVANTAGES OF MEDICINE

The people
As a doctor, you will rarely be lonely. You will spend your life working in a team of like-minded and motivated individuals, all working towards the same aims as you. The busyness and pressure of the job means that everyone, including you, will consistently perform to a high level, and this makes the experience of working in such a team incredibly rewarding.

Lifelong learning
A career in medicine means finding a passion and being able to continually expand your knowledge in this field. You will have opportunities to discuss ideas with like-minded colleagues, continually challenging and teaching each other. This ensures you are constantly stimulated and interested.

9

A wide range of job opportunities

The majority of doctors stay in clinical practice. This could mean specialising in an area such as cardiology, general surgery, a specialised form of bariatric surgery, or another field such as paediatrics or obstetrics and gynaecology.

However, clinical practice isn't the only route you can follow with a degree in medicine. Doctors may carry out research, work for pharmaceutical companies and law practices, or use their vast array of skills to be successful in many other fields of work.

Variety

As a doctor, every day is different. Although the days may consist of regular features such as ward rounds or clinics, the patients will be different, the diagnoses and treatments will change, and you may have to deal with emergency situations. This constant variety ensures you are continually interested and challenged.

Job security and flexibility

There is no place in the world that doesn't need doctors: as a result, a medical career is both secure and flexible. With the right forward planning, you can work anywhere in the world.

Great days

Although becoming a doctor is hard work, there will be days when you see all of the hard work pay off. This could be the day when you finally solve a differential diagnosis, or when a decision you make helps a patient recover. It could be a smaller success such as managing to take blood from a patient when numerous others haven't been successful. It could be a day when a patient or family member offers you their warmest thanks, or when they return for a follow-up and you see how well they are doing.

Making a difference

Although it may seem like a cliché, being a doctor does give you the opportunity to make a difference to the lives of others. There are few careers that give the job satisfaction or sense of purpose that being a doctor provides.

DISADVANTAGES OF MEDICINE

Many exams

Lifelong learning requires lifelong reading – and a lot of exams. If beginning medical school at age 18, you will continue to sit important exams for fifteen years or more. Even after these are completed, you will have to demonstrate your commitment to learning and keeping yourself up-todate through the process of revalidation every five years.

Stress

Being a doctor can be a stressful career. Doctors have to see numerous patients and juggle multiple important jobs at the same time as dealing with nurses and other colleagues asking for help. You have to learn how to prioritise and stay motivated; you often won't get a lunch break or be able to leave on time, which may mean missing events with family and friends. More significantly, doctors have to make decisions about life and death. There will be many sleepless nights, not just because of the night shifts, but also because it can be hard to switch off – you may worry about a patient or a decision you have made.

Every doctor has had days when they have cried or wanted to run away. These could be days when you have more work than you can possibly complete, or when you are unsure of a diagnosis or a decision. Similarly, it can be emotionally difficult if a patient dies, or when a patient or their family member takes out their anger on you.

Pay

Despite many students' preconceptions, medicine isn't a career you should choose for purely financial reasons. There are many other better-paid careers, and although in the long term a doctor's salary is high, there are many years of training before this stage. Furthermore, the length of time needed to qualify can lead to a lot of student debt, which is a factor worth bearing in mind.

HOW CAN I DECIDE WHETHER MEDICINE IS THE RIGHT CAREER FOR ME?

The points above paint a realistic picture of the life of a doctor. No career choice has advantages alone, but you need to ensure that you care enough about the profession to cope with the harder elements of being a doctor.

There are also more practical things you will need to do in order to make an informed decision about medicine as a career. Work experience, in particular, is essential. The more you can witness and experience the everyday life of a doctor, the better equipped you will be to make your decision.

Many students carry out work experience with consultants, attending clinics and ward rounds; as the majority of your career will be spent at consultant level, seeing the daily schedule and stresses is a great source of information. Furthermore, if you already have thoughts about a speciality which interests you, learning more about the field may influence your decision.

However, it is a long road and a steep learning curve before you become a consultant. It is essential that you experience life as a junior doctor as well, to learn how difficult the first few years can be. Following a junior doctor during a series of shifts including regular days, on-call shifts and night shifts will be invaluable in giving you a realistic picture of life as a doctor. Speaking to the juniors, hearing their thoughts and seeing their routines will help you make this difficult decision.

To make a fully informed decision, it is also important to keep up with current affairs surrounding the medical profession. For instance, reading about the problems facing the NHS and the recent disputes around the junior doctor contract may influence your decision as to whether this is the profession for you. Remember that although your school, your family members and doctors or healthcare professionals you meet will all have opinions on whether you should apply for Medicine, it is essential that you make the decision that is right for you.

During a career in medicine, the great days and the difficult days will help you to become a stronger person and an even better doctor. Being able to make a difference every day is the greatest advantage of a career in medicine, and if you are certain this is the career for you, you have a very exciting future ahead.

The next chapter examines the first part of this journey – from making the decision to apply to medical school, to the various parts of the application process and what you can then expect from a medical degree.

1 FROM DECISION TO DOCTOR

From Decision to Doctor

Choosing what to study at university is a big decision, and selecting the path of medicine has its own host of challenges. In this chapter we'll run through the various steps to take, from choosing your subjects at school and completing the UCAS application, through to being a medical student and finally graduating. It is a long process, and while it may seem daunting and arduous at times, the joy of becoming a doctor is undeniable and will hopefully make all those hours in the library seem worth it in the end.

SCHOOL
A deep love of science is necessary for any doctor. It helps you get through the dense lectures on biochemistry and pharmacokinetics in medical school and, crucially, to understand why some patients are sicker than others and why some drugs fundamentally work.

Academically, a good applicant will have performed well at GCSEs and be on-track for at least some A grades at A Level. Many medical schools specify what they want you to have studied at A Level: this can include Biology, Chemistry, Mathematics, Physics, and one "contrasting" subject like German or Geography.

The rationale behind the contrasting subject is similar to that behind being part of the school choir or rugby team. The experiences and qualities acquired can make you an interesting person and supposedly a better doctor. Being able to work with others in a team and having good interpersonal skills is as important in captaining a sports team as it is when leading a ward round. Being able to juggle sports, music, academics and volunteering demonstrates time management skills that will be invaluable at university, and also shows that you can maintain the ever-elusive "work-life balance".

DECIDING IF MEDICINE IS FOR YOU
If you've always been a person that likes both science and working with people, it is likely that you have at some point considered applying for Medicine. There are many pros and cons to consider, and it's important to see and ask as much as you can about both the training and the job.

Chapter 2 takes you through the advantages and disadvantages of the profession, and how you can decide whether medicine is the right career path for you.

If you decide that medicine isn't for you, remember that this is a perfectly valid choice! Some people are turned off by the scientific demands, the patient contact, the long study or the poor pay at junior level, to name only a few reasons. There are also many other related careers that you might also consider, such as nursing, biomedical research, dentistry, public health and policy, and health administration. Another option if you are unsure about pursuing medicine is to apply for another subject, and consider applying for Graduate Entry Medicine once you graduate.

CHOOSING WHERE TO GO
Once you've decided to apply for Medicine, the next step is choosing where to apply. There are about 30 different medical schools in the UK and they all teach medicine in a slightly different way. Some courses focus on a 'pre-clinical vs clinical' division of study; some have an 'intercalated' year where you get an extra Bachelor's degree (usually in Physiology or a related area). Some use problem-based learning, while others are more traditionally didactic with lectures and practicals.

Selecting the right course for you is important, but another factor to consider is location. Do you want to be on a campus or in a city? Do you want to be near home or far away? What is the clinical base for your university – will you be sent across the neighbouring counties, or mainly to a city centre?

Take your time researching different universities online, and go on as many open days as you feel you need to. (A list of medical schools and their requirements can be found in Appendix 1.) Remember that you are choosing where to spend five or six years of your life: it is not a decision to take lightly.

UCAS
The UCAS form is what you will fill out in the autumn of upper Sixth Form, and is your first chance to demonstrate why you deserve a place to study Medicine at one of the universities you have chosen. Medicine is a very competitive course, so it is essential that the whole of your

application is as strong as possible.

In the UCAS form, you'll be asked to fill in your personal details and qualifications, and submit a Personal Statement and school reference. As well as a good academic record, you also need to have a range of medical experiences to draw upon. These can form a part of the Personal Statement, which is the cornerstone of the UCAS application.

WORK EXPERIENCE AND VOLUNTEERING
Some medical schools will specify on their websites the exact amount or type of medical work experience they expect from applicants, but the following is a summary of what they are generally looking for:

Reflections on interactions seen between doctors, patients and other healthcare workers.
* An experience in a primary healthcare setting – e.g. a GP practice.
* An experience in a specialist secondary (or tertiary/quaternary) healthcare setting – i.e. a hospital.
* A long-term and/or short-term volunteering commitment with different potentially vulnerable populations;
    – Children
    – People with disabilities
    – The elderly
    – People in mental distress
    – Refugees
    – Homeless people
* A working knowledge of the NHS: the current political climate, the roles of the different members of a Multidisciplinary Team and so on.
* Research experience: particularly helpful if applying to a scientific course like Oxbridge, Imperial, UCL or St Andrews.
* Teaching experience: for example, at a youth club or primary school. Many doctors are involved in teaching at the medical school attached to their hospital, so this is something you will probably become involved in after you qualify – getting some teaching experience now is beneficial.
* Managerial experience: many doctors are also managers of a team or involved in wider healthcare provision, so this can prove helpful in your later career.

Find out more about obtaining work experience and how to make the best of it in Chapter 4.

PERSONAL STATEMENT

This is an opportunity for you to convince medical schools of why you deserve a place in 4000 characters or less. It should cover a range of ideas:

1. Why you are interested in a career in medicine – for example, did a specific life event trigger your interest?
2. Why you are academically suited to medicine – academic achievements, prizes, research experience, and success at any national/international competitions.
3. Your own research on medicine as a career – this covers work experience, going to lectures, talking to medical professionals, and reading books on topics of interest.
4. Extra-curricular activities that relate to the skills needed to be a doctor – for example, clinical work experience, organisational skills in volunteering or a job, and leadership/teamwork in e.g. sports or music.
5. Why you are a well-rounded individual – essentially, demonstrate that you are more than a medical robot!

The Personal Statement is one of the harder aspects of the application, and it takes a long time to write (and rewrite) a version that both you and your parents / teachers / tutors are happy with. Don't be discouraged when you're writing the fifteenth draft! The best way to approach the Personal Statement is to start gaining those experiences early – read medical books during your GCSEs and organise work experience for the holidays.

You can read more about developing your Personal Statement in Chapter 5.

ADMISSIONS TESTS

There are three admissions tests for medical schools in the UK, and different universities have different requirements. It is worth looking at which test universities require, if any, and how much weight they put on it when considering your application. This can help determine where to apply, and a savvy applicant may adapt their choices based on how they're expected to perform.

You can find out more about the detail of these tests in Chapter 6. In brief:

The BMAT has 3 sections:
- **Section 1** tests your Problem Solving, Understanding Argument and Data Analysis & Inference skills.
- **Section 2** tests your scientific ability.
- **Section 3** tests your ability to structure a cohesive and succinct argument in essay format.

The UCAT has 5 sections:
- **Verbal Reasoning** – tests your ability to understand written information.
- **Decision Making** – tests your ability to make sound decisions and judgments using complex information.
- **Quantitative Reasoning** – tests your ability to perform calculations.
- **Abstract Reasoning** – tests your convergent and divergent thinking to infer relationships from information.
- **Situational Judgement** – tests your ability to understand realworld situations and identify appropriate management.

The GAMSAT has 3 sections and is mainly for graduate applicants:
- **Reasoning in Humanities and Social Sciences** – tests your ability to understand and interpret ideas in social and cultural contexts.
- **Written Communication** – tests your ability to develop and produce ideas in writing.
- **Reasoning in Biological and Physical Sciences** – tests your knowledge and aptitude in biology, chemistry and physics.

Each of these tests is used by admissions departments in a different way. Some universities will place great weight on them; others will only use them to help determine who is to be invited to interview. You can prepare for these tests by working through past questions, which are available online as well as in certain books. The more practise you complete, the more confident you will feel and the better you are likely to perform.

INTERVIEW

If your application passes the first round, your university may call you for interview.

Each medical school conducts interviews slightly differently – which is something you can specifically prepare for – but there are some general themes. In chapter 8 we will discuss how to approach interview questions in more depth.

Below are some of the different styles that questions can come in:
- **Multiple Mini Interview (MMI)** – here you will circulate around a room of different stations, all of which assess your fitness to be a doctor. Different scenarios assess your ability to communicate complicated information, demonstrate empathy, or make difficult decisions.
- **Ethics question** – you may be asked to assess a situation and outline how you would make a difficult ethical choice as a doctor or a layperson.
- **Personal Statement** – anything on your Personal Statement or further application documents is 'fair game' for questions. Make sure you have read everything you say you have.
- **Medical questions** – you may be asked to talk about your knowledge of the NHS, hospital work experience, or something about a patient experience you may have had.
- **Scientific questions** – you may be asked to explain a scientific concept you have come across at school or in work experience.
- **Personal questions** – the interviewers may want to learn more about you as an individual or ask what you do in your spare time.

There are no guarantees about who will interview you: it may be a panel or an individual. Often, there are both doctors and laypeople involved in the interview process, and each interview is designed to help you perform to the best of your ability.

UNIVERSITY

You have been accepted to medical school! Congratulations! Now begins the really hard work. At university, you'll begin to learn the foundations of medical science, and over the course of your degree, build this up to become a truly competent doctor. The courses all vary, but here are the general overarching structures in which you will be taught.

LECTURES

Every medical school has lectures for their students. You and the other 200 people in your academic year will sit and listen to doctors and scientists for up to six hours a day. This will remain the same throughout medical school – whether you're learning the mechanism of muscular contraction or the differential diagnosis of chest pain. Everyone attends lectures in different ways: some people take a laptop and record everything verbatim, some slouch at the back with a pen and pad, and others watch the lecture podcast from home.

PRACTICALS

Most medical schools punctuate the lectures with practical sessions – either teaching scientific techniques like pipetting, clinical skills such as taking blood pressure readings, or illustrating something from a recent lecture (for example, using frog muscle and contraction to calculate myofibrillar length).

GROUP LEARNING

Lots of medical schools believe in students teaching themselves and so set up schemes like Problem-based learning (PBL), where students research a topic each week and then teach it to the rest of the class. This continues lifelong in medicine, with doctors often teaching those around them.

CLINICAL EXPOSURE

The beginning of medical school can seem quite dry with a lot of lectures and book learning, but many newer medical schools also intersperse a day or two of clinical contact per week. This is a way to ground the science that you are learning, and to remind you why you applied to medical school in the first place. It's also a good way to learn how hospitals and clinics run – every single one is different, and navigating them as a junior doctor is easier the more exposure you get.

FITNESS TO PRACTISE

In addition to building up your scientific knowledge, medical school is there to educate and prepare you for the day-to-day life of a doctor. You need to understand the ethics surrounding signing a DNACPR ("Do Not Attempt Cardio-Pulmonary Resuscitation"), not just where to ask the consultant to sign it.

UNION

Medics are notoriously rowdy, and many medical school student unions are very active, with societies and socials for the freshers to join. You can continue your passionate love affair with rugby, or pick up a new sport like Mixed Netball. The social life in the medical school student unions is vibrant with something for everyone to participate in. You will form very close friendships with the other medical students in virtue of the amount of time you spend together on the course, and this continues right through your career.

CLINICAL

Once you properly start the clinical phase of medical school, the course shifts from a classroom to a clinical focus. Instead of days of lectures throughout the year, you will be assigned a senior doctor to follow on various rotations, being expected to learn the diagnostic and practical skills of a doctor in hospital and supplemented by your reading outside hours. This is when you begin to specifically learn 'specialties' such as paediatrics, cardiology, colorectal surgery, psychiatry, obstetrics and gynaecology, and rheumatology.

WARDS

You will be taught how to interact with patients on wards, including skills such as how to take a history, how to take blood, and how to interpret an X-ray. These skills are honed after years of practise, and the more time you spend in clinical contact the better you will be.

THEATRE

There is a broad divide between medicine and surgery, and at medical school you must learn both. The majority of a consultant surgeon's time is spent in the operating theatre, and medical students are often invited to join them. A knowledge of the exact procedure is not necessary. Instead, they want to see a willingness to get involved, and an appreciation of what has brought that patient to theatre – why Brenda the 86-year-old woman has fallen, and how her osteoporosis has contributed to her total hip replacement operation today.

CLINICS
You will be allocated clinic times where you may go and sit with a consultant or registrar and observe their clinic. In doing so you will see a range of clinical styles: the idea is that at the end of medical school you will have developed your own manner of talking to patients, with which you both build a rapport and discover the necessary information to diagnose and treat them.

MISCELLANEOUS
The healthcare profession is very varied, and as a medical student you are in the position to see all the highly specialised jobs that a junior doctor never will as part of their role. There are many jobs in and around the hospital that your medical school might assign you to. For example, on a day with a community midwife you'll go around the practice with her, helping deliver babies or do post-natal checks. With the diabetic specialist nurse you might finesse your blood-taking and check 30 people's HbA1Cs. At a GP practice, you can help administer the annual flu vaccine with the practice nurse.

OSCES AND EXAMS
Throughout your clinical years you will sit two types of exams – the standard written papers (often multiple-choice) that assess how much you have actually learnt over the year, and a practical exam called an OSCE. In order to graduate, you must pass both these sets of exams.
These exams use fake patients, and ask you to perform a simple task in either 5 or 10 minutes. This may range from cannulating a patient to performing an examination of their respiratory system or explaining the results of a woman's recent UTI test. Their scope is endless, and medical students notoriously fear these exams – although they needn't as long as they know how to communicate with a patient!

FIRST JOB ON THE WARD
Well done! You've graduated from medical school!
Now you begin your first job as the F1 on the Hepato-Pancreato-Biliary Surgery team, looking after all the patients post-surgery and making

23

sure their bloods don't rapidly deteriorate. You are fully part of the team now, and everyone has your back. The job will be tough, but you'll be able to go home every day knowing that you have learnt something new, and that you've helped a bunch of people.

2 WORK EXPERIENCE & VOLUNTEERING

WORK EXPERIENCE & VOLUNTEERING

In this chapter we will discuss the practicalities of finding work experience and volunteering placements. More important, however, is the question of what you should be looking to gain from this experience in order to make the most of it in your application to medical school.

WHY DO I NEED WORK EXPERIENCE?

The main reason for doing work experience in medicine is to get a first-hand understanding of what a doctor's life actually looks like. Hospitals are grossly misrepresented on television and in film: what may, on Grey's Anatomy, seem like a 5-minute kidney transplant is in reality much more complex and lengthy. At no point do you see the 45 minutes of anaesthetics induction and preparation; the 20 minutes spent scrubbing up and preparing for incision; or the four hours dissecting down the arteries and veins to prepare the transplant – not to mention the week of post-operative care and the complications and check-ups implicit in taking lifelong medication. If you're applying for Medicine then it's your duty to thoroughly educate yourself before you start down that career path.

Another benefit of work experience is the opportunity to learn about the current structure of the NHS and how the political climate is affecting those on the front line of healthcare. You will also gain other insights, such as basic knowledge of the various roles in a multidisciplinary team or the rationale behind the 'bare below the elbow' rule, that are hard to obtain from just reading.

Work experience is a way for you to see the other side of medicine and learn directly from senior medical professionals. Volunteering placements come in a variety of formats: some may be longer-term, or may give you a chance to get more involved in talking to clients or service users. As a result, students will have slightly different learning experiences.

Apart from the opportunity to learn from experts, medical schools also recommend work experience as a way to gain repeated exposure to institutions where care is being given to people in need. This can take many different forms, but bear in mind what is most relevant to a career in medicine. While it is altruistic to be volunteering in an Oxfam bookshop and honing your communication skills with tricky customers, it pales in comparison to what you could learn as an assistant at a care facility for those with disabilities.

On these placements, you are likely to develop key medical skills and attributes such as empathy and active listening. This is important, as it is rare that you'll be able to have actual patient contact on work experience placements. You are likely to shadow a doctor and observe their daily work, but most trusts are not happy for a sixth-former to be talking to patients alone. On volunteering placements there is sometimes the opportunity to get more hands-on experience: once you have been trained and worked at the facility a few times, your role can grow based on your ability. Practical learning experiences – such as playing with a child with a developmental disability, or understanding more about the course of Parkinson's from talking to someone in a care home – are invaluable in helping you to develop your interests as a medical applicant.

It's a privilege to be allowed to observe a hospital for a week, and you will gain an insight into patients' lives that many will never see. Your reflections on your experiences will be a key component of your Personal Statement and can make a strong candidate stand out. These experiences are also invaluable to discuss at an interview, so the more that you can see and hear, the more you will have to talk about. You should be able to draw on a series of patient-doctor interactions, and comment on both what went well and what you might consider doing differently.

WHAT KIND OF WORK EXPERIENCE DO I NEED?

Some universities specify on their website what experience they require their applicants to have, whilst others are more flexible and just give general suggestions. Overall, the more experience you can get, the better. You need to find a balance between the number of placements you take and the depth to which you are embedded in each one. While you need to see a range of medical practice, it is of limited benefit if you are only gaining a superficial understanding of the profession. In any case, the amount of work experience most students do is usually limited by practicalities; your experience will be predominantly limited to your holidays from school, and placements can be difficult to sort out.

A good aim is to have completed at least the following by the time of writing your Personal Statement – both to demonstrate the necessary dedication to the caring professions and medicine specifically, and to give you relevant experiences to write about:

- One week of experience in a primary healthcare setting – e.g. a GP surgery.
- 2x one-week experiences in a secondary (or tertiary/quaternary) healthcare setting – i.e. a hospital.
- A long-term (>1 year) volunteering commitment with a potentially vulnerable population:
  - Children
  - People with disabilities
  - The elderly
  - People in mental distress
  - Refugees
  - Homeless people
- A short-term volunteering placement with a different demographic.

RESEARCH, TEACHING AND MANAGEMENT

Research, teaching and management are the three key extracurricular areas in which every doctor, from juniors to consultants, will continue to hone their skills throughout their career. Although not as essential as the work experience and volunteering placements, finding a way to make your Saturday job fit into one of these categories will strengthen your application.

At any stage in medicine, you will be able to get involved in research, and it can be central in climbing the professional ladder. If you're considering a career in research from the outset, and are applying to a university where the course is very academic (such as Oxford or Cambridge), experience in a laboratory could prove very beneficial; it will also help you decide whether you are suited to this kind of course. Many doctors qualify and later move away from clinical work to focus on lab research. On a work experience placement, you may be able to do more in a lab than you would on a ward: the placements can be longer, and most labs are happy to take someone on and train them up to do the jobs that no one else has time to do.

Due to the highly integrated relationship between medical schools and teaching hospitals, doctors are all expected to devote some time to teaching. Being a good educator should come naturally to doctors, as the job depends on the ability to communicate effectively with patients and colleagues. Having some experience as a tutor, classroom assistant or teacher for any age group is worthwhile, and has the bonus of potential payment.

Doctors all work as part of a team throughout their career, both as the leader and as a team player. In addition to the mountains of bureaucracy and administration in the NHS, many consultants also develop a business in the private sphere. Experience of healthcare administration and being in a managerial position is therefore also very helpful. This can be gained from working as a secretary in a clinical practice, or from shadowing medico-legal work.

If you are considering having a gap year, you have the luxury of time, and you can use this wisely. One role to consider is that of a Healthcare Assistant (HCA). These are individuals who work in a hospital or clinic without a formal medical or nursing degree, and help the whole organisation run smoothly. The role offers a unique insight into the workings of a clinical service, and offers practical clinical experience that is second to none.

Below are some possible volunteering placements to help you think about what you might enjoy doing. If you find a cause that you are passionate about, both you and the organisation in question will benefit more:
• Soup kitchen
• Fundraising centre
• Care home

Helpline (e.g. Childline)
• Mentoring programme
• Local primary school
• Community centre
• Play group
• Charity shop
• Air ambulance

- Prisoner support service
- Respite care home
- Hospital ward volunteer – AKA 'Candystripers'

It is easier to write a Personal Statement if you have certain areas of interest that you have cultivated and can demonstrate through your work experience, reading or other activities such as attending lectures. It's rare that a medical school will ask you to be an expert on cirrhosis if you sat in on a liver clinic or read a hepatology article, but the more knowledge you have before your placement in that area of medicine, the more you will get out of it.

If you are unsure where your interests lie, below are some of the general systems in the body and areas of medical interest that you might specifically seek experience in:

- Cardiology & Cardiovascular surgery
- Global health
- Respiratory & Tuberculosis
- Emergency and Acute medicine
- Trauma and Orthopaedics
- Gastroenterology & HPB and Colorectal surgery
- Geriatrics
- Rheumatology
- Endocrinology and Diabetes
- Paediatrics
- Renal medicine and Hepatology
- Psychiatry
- Obstetrics, Gynaecology and Breast
- Public health and policy
- Plastic surgery
- Oncology and Palliative care

WHERE SHOULD I VOLUNTEER OR GET WORK EXPERIENCE?

Many students will arrange volunteering placements near their school or home – particularly placements they are returning to regularly. Charitable organisations usually have branches across the country, and you will generally be able to find somewhere convenient to you. There are several websites that look to connect volunteers with organisations that need assistance, such as www.do-it.org, which you can use to help find something near you.

The most common way for students to obtain a work experience placement is through a personal connection, whether local or further afield. Don't be afraid to ask for help in this situation: remember that every doctor had to seek work experience when they applied to medical school, so they know it can be difficult. You could also contact those you know in allied healthcare professions: a day at their own work can be just as useful an experience. They may also have their own contacts to whom they would be happy to introduce you – nurses, pharmacists and scientists are good examples.

There are many possible specialities in which you could secure a work experience placement, but this will greatly depend on whom you know (or who you can petition by email!). Even if you aren't interested in the liver, it is still definitely worthwhile gaining a week of work experience with your uncle in hepatology. Some ideas of contacts you could use include:
- Friends of the family
- Parents of school friends
- Neighbours
- Extended family

An old student of your school
- Through your school University Advisor's contacts
- Your own doctor

If you have used up every connection you have, or want something a bit different, you should get in contact with your local hospitals and healthcare services. They will be used to having students request a work experience placement, and some will have a scheme to accommodate you. If you haven't received a response after two weeks, it is worth following up, although you should be careful not to bombard them.

WORK EXPERIENCE ABROAD
Some applicants also seek placements abroad. This can look good as long you make a considered and intelligent point out of the experience. It is much better to be able make a comparison between the pressure on the junior doctors in Tanzania vs those in the UK, rather than just write

about seeing a patient with tuberculosis on holiday in Ghana.

Having said that, placements or trips abroad may allow you to see conditions and illnesses that you would never come across in the UK. Witnessing healthcare in a less economically developed country can underline how fortunate we are in the UK – both in our general quality of life, and with our healthcare system.

As in the UK, the amount of practical clinical experience you can gain is quite limited for reasons of liability, insurance and patient safety. Such trips can end up very costly, particularly if organised by a specialist company, and so it may be hard to justify the expense when there is limited benefit.

WHEN SHOULD I DO IT?

It is best to start organising work experience as soon as you begin considering an application for Medicine. Not only will it help you to decide whether it is the right path for you, but also, as you have read, organising a placement can take time. To make effective use of the time you have, it is important to be organised and plan how you are going to fit everything in before you apply.

Time is relatively limited if you consider how much you want to have accomplished by the autumn of Year 13. After completing GCSEs, you will only have four long holidays in which to organise work experience – the summers after Year 11 and Year 12, and the Christmas and Easter holidays in Year 12. You may be fortunate and also have long half-terms in which to organise a placement, but remember that holidays are also a time for you to consolidate your learning from school, and that you may have public or mock exams upon your return.

If you know you want to pursue a Medicine application, it is possible to start work experience before your GCSEs: however, some hospitals may have a minimum age requirement and so may decline your requests until after you have turned 16.

Organising work experience can take a lot of time, emailing and patience. It is one of the stages of the process that many students and parents complain about, and with good cause. Administrators may not respond; your emails may be bounced around a department; and you may end up being given a placement in an area you have no interest in. However, if you are truly dedicated to medicine you have to persevere and try not to be demoralised.

HOW TO ORGANISE THE PLACEMENT

Every placement will be different, and organising each one will very much depend on how you arranged it. However, below are some general tips to remember when organising and preparing for placements:
Try and organise your placements as far in advance as possible.
Exploit every personal connection available.

Check the websites of local charities or healthcare centres for information on placements.

Make connections when on a placement to see if anyone else might offer to take you on as a work experience student at a later date.

Some places may ask for a DBS check. This takes a while to process and involves a lot of paperwork, so get it done as soon as you are told about it.

Some places ask for an application form to be completed and may call you for an interview. Prepare for these, and make sure the application form is completed to the best of your ability – you may be directly competing with other students for the placement.

- Profusely thank anyone who helps you get a placement – they will be more likely to help you (or another student in your situation) again. Chocolates and bottles of wine are always appreciated on a ward.
- Get experience in a range of disciplines and see what comparisons you can make between them.
- Remember that you will be expected to abide by the rules of the organisation giving you the placement – whether these are professional guidelines such as confidentiality or a dress code – so ensure that you are aware of this before your placement begins.

ON THE PLACEMENT

Once you've secured a placement, the next thing to consider is what to do during your placement and how to make the most of it.

When you begin the placement, you are likely to be given a timetable or at least an idea of what you will be doing there. The best thing to do is throw yourself into the experience and get as immersed as possible in the profession.

You should have been told what to wear, but general guidance in a hospital is to wear something smart but comfortable, and to remain bare below the elbows. For men this is usually a shirt (without tie, sleeves rolled up) and suit trousers or chinos. For women this translates as a smart dress, or a blouse and skirt or trouser combination. Jeans and trainers are generally not permitted in healthcare settings, and 'bare below the elbows' means no watches, bracelets or rings. Hair for both genders should be tied up neatly. This dress code may not apply to volunteering placements, but check with your contact before arriving.

During your placement, you are likely to experience a lot of different situations, and it can be hard to remember everything by the time your medical school interview comes around. It is a good idea to try and write about your experience at the end of each day, so you can reflect on everything you have seen and done. While the medical details of the disease you may have seen are important, just as vital are the little nuances of behaviour that have stayed with you – for example, how the doctor moderated her behaviour when dealing with a partially deaf man, or how the nurse placed her hand on the patient's shoulder when she was clearly becoming a bit distressed. It is just as useful to make notes on things that you were impressed by as it is to record things that surprised, shocked or upset you. When doing this, you should maintain total confidentiality, and not commit anything to writing that could potentially identify a patient.

In your interview, medical schools will be looking for you to not merely describe what you saw and did, but to be able to reflect on it and consider how you might behave in that situation if you were the doctor. Thinking about this aspect as you go along will help you to discuss it in more depth in an interview setting.

This interview method represents a recent move in the medical profession towards something called 'reflective practice'. The idea is that doctors need to be more self-aware in their practice, and constantly re-evaluate themselves to ensure they are providing the best possible standard of care. Doctors do this by using a process where you describe and look at what you did, consider what you were thinking and feeling about that event, evaluate what was good or bad about the experience and analyse and rationalise the overall situation. You can then draw a conclusion about what else you could have done differently, and construct an action plan to improve your performance in the future.

If you are conscientious and write down notes about your placement, trying to analyse it with a 'reflective' lens, then you should be able to make the most of your experience. The next chapter will look at one of the main ways you can give an Admissions Tutor a sense of this: the Personal Statement.

All universities for a degree in medicine will require a criminal record check and a satisfactory health screening assessment.

3 CHOOSING YOUR UNIVERSITIES

Aberdeen

COURSE: A 5 year course with the option of a 6 year course with an intercalated degree to gain a Bachelor of Science degree in Medical Sciences
The course offers clinical exposure in the first year but most clinical exposure in later years
GRADES: AAA
Applicants must study A Level Chemistry and one subject from Biology/ Human Biology, Maths and Physics
GCSEs: A combination of Grade A/7 & B/6 grades is essential especially in science subjects. A minimum of grade C/5 in English and Maths is required
ADMISSIONS TEST: UCAT
INTERVIEW: Multiple Mini Interviews
LOCATION: Campus university with clinical attachments in surrounding areas. Option to experience a remote and rural medicine programme
RELATED SUBJECTS: Microbiology, Biochemistry
INTERNATIONAL STUDENTS: Accepted

Anglia Ruskin

COURSE: A 5 year degree programme which is full time and leads to a Primary Medical Qualification that will allow graduates to register with the GMC.
GRADES: AAA
GCSEs: 5 GCSE grades at grade A-C (9-4), including English Language, Maths and two science subjects.
ADMISSIONS TEST: UCAT
INTERVIEW: Multiple Mini Interviews
LOCATION: Campus university based in Chelmsford.
RELATED SUBJECTS: Biomedical Science with Foundation Year BSC (Hons), Medical Science BSc (Hons)
INTERNATIONAL STUDENTS: Accepted

Aston

COURSE: A 5 year degree programme.
The course offers clinical exposure from the first year but more in later years.
GRADES: AAA – AAB, must have Chemistry and Biology at A Level.
GCSEs: A minimum of five GCSEs/IGCSEs at grade B / grade 6 or above, which must include English language, Mathematics, Chemistry, Biology or double science.
ADMISSIONS TEST: UCAT
INTERVIEW: Multiple Mini Interviews
LOCATION: Based in Birmingham.
RELATED SUBJECTS: Biomedical Science (Hons), Pharmacy MPharm (Hons)
INTERNATIONAL STUDENTS: Accepted

Birmingham

COURSE: A 5 year course with the option of 6 years to intercalate to get an additional degree
The course offers clinical exposure from the first year but more in later years.
GRADES: A*AA
Applicants must study A Level Biology and Chemistry
GCSEs: 7 GCSES at a minimum of grade B/6 including English Language, English Literature, Mathematics and Sciences
ADMISSIONS TEST: UCAT
INTERVIEW: Multiple Mini Interviews including a station where you will be assessed on basic calculations
LOCATION: Campus university with clinical attachments in surrounding areas
RELATED SUBJECTS: Medical Sciences, Medical Biochemistry
INTERNATIONAL STUDENTS: Accepted

Brighton and Sussex

COURSE: A 5 year course with an option of a 6 year course to intercalate
The course offers clinical experience from the first year with more exposure in later years
GRADES: AAA
Applicants must offer A Level Biology and Chemistry
GCSEs: A minimum of grade B/6 in Maths and English Language or English Literature
ADMISSION TEST: BMAT
INTERVIEW: Multiple Mini Interviews
LOCATION: Two universities, campus based with clinical attachments in surrounding areas
RELATED SUBJECTS: Brighton University – Biomedical Sciences Biological Sciences, Sussex University – Biomedical Science, Medical Neuroscience
INTERNATIONAL STUDENTS: Accepted

Bristol

COURSE: A 5 year course with an option of 6 years if you choose to study for an intercalated degree to gain a BSc. There is also the option to do a 6 year course, MB ChB Gateway to Medicine for students from specific schools/colleges who do not meet the academic requirements.
The course offers clinical exposure from the first year but most clinical exposure in later years
GRADES: AAA
Applicants must study A Level Chemistry and another lab-based science
GCSEs: A minimum of five GCSEs at grade A/7 to include Mathematics, English Language and two science subjects
ADMISSIONS TEST: UCAT
INTERVIEW: Multiple Mini Interviews
Prior to the interview applicants are required to complete a form which documents the type and duration of the work experience they have carried out
LOCATION: Campus university with clinical attachments in surrounding areas
RELATED SUBJECTS: Physiological Science, Medical Microbiology
INTERNATIONAL STUDENTS: Accepted

Buckingham

COURSE: A unique course in the UK which lasts 4.5 years and commences study in January rather than the typical September start date
The course offers clinical exposure from first year but more in later years
GRADES: AAB
The applicant must study A Level Chemistry and one from Maths or Biology. If Biology is not studied at A Level it must be studied at GCSE Level or equivalent.
GCSEs: A minimum of grade C/5 in English and Maths
INTERVIEW: Objective, Structured Selection Examination (OSSE) which are similar to Multiple Mini Interviews
LOCATION: Campus university with attachments in surrounding areas
RELATED SUBJECTS: None similar
INTERNATIONAL STUDENTS: Accepted
The fees the same for UK and international applicants

Cambridge

COURSE: A six year course gaining a BA after three years, however you have to reapply after 3 years to study clinical medicine at Cambridge or you can move to a different university to study this.
The first two years are science based with the third year being spent in a subject you have chosen. The final three years are clinical based.
GRADES: A*A*A*
Applicants must study A Level Chemistry and one from Biology, Physics or Mathematics. However, most applicants have at least three science/mathematics A Levels and some Colleges require this or have requirements for particular subjects. It is important to visit individual college websites for details on this
GCSEs: A minimum of grade C/5 in GCSE Double Award Science and Mathematics
ADMISSIONS TEST: BMAT
INTERVIEW: Traditional Interview
LOCATION: College system for pre-clinical studies, variety of attachments in different hospitals in surrounding areas for clinical medicine
RELATED SUBJECTS: Natural Sciences, Psychological and Behavioural Sciences
INTERNATIONAL STUDENTS: Accepted

Cardiff

COURSE: A 5 year course with the option of 6 years to intercalate to gain a BSc
The course offers clinical experience from the first year but more in later years
GRADES: AAA
Applicants must offer A Level Chemistry and Biology with a pass in the separate practical component
GCSEs: A minimum of grade B/6 in Mathematics and English Language. For GCSE separate sciences grades of AAB are required in any combination in Biology, Chemistry and Physics and for double science grades of AA are required.
ADMISSIONS TEST: UCAT
INTERVIEW: No information on website but in previous years has been more traditional style of interview
LOCATION: Campus university with clinical attachments throughout Wales
RELATED SUBJECTS: Medical Pharmacology, Biomedical Sciences, Biological Sciences
INTERNATIONAL STUDENTS: Accepted

Dundee

COURSE: A 5 year course with an option of a 6 year course with an intercalated degree to gain a BMSc
The course offers clinical exposure in the first year but most clinical exposure in later years
GRADES: AAA
Applicants must study A-Level Chemistry and one other science subject
GCSEs: No minimum grades are specified, however achievements at GCSE will be taken into account
ADMISSIONS TEST: UCAT required
INTERVIEW: Multiple Mini Interviews
LOCATION: Campus university with clinical attachments in surrounding areas
RELATED SUBJECTS: Medical Sciences, Nursing
INTERNATIONAL STUDENTS: Accepted

East Anglia/Norwich

COURSE: A 5 year course but option of 6 years to intercalate to gain a master's degree
The course offers clinical exposure from the first month of studying but more in later years
GRADES: AAA
The applicant must study A Level Biology/Human Biology and either Physics or Chemistry including a pass in the practical element
GCSEs: A minimum of 6 GCSEs at grade A/7 to include English, Mathematics and two Science subjects
ADMISSIONS TEST: UCAT
INTERVIEW: Multiple Mini Interviews
LOCATION: Campus university with clinical attachments in surrounding areas
RELATED SUBJECTS: BSc Paramedic Science, variety of Nursing degrees
INTERNATIONAL STUDENTS: Accepted

Edge Hill

COURSE: First intake is September 2020. This course will be available for application from September 2019, subject to University validation and GMC approval.
A 5 year course which leads to the award of a MBChB primary medical qualification. Students from under represented backgrounds across thr North West of England who do not meet the acaemic grade requirements can take a 1 year Foundation course. Upon achieving the pass mark they may then start the 5 year degree.
GRADES: TBC
GCSEs: TBC
ADMISSIONS TEST: TBC
INTERVIEW: TBC
LOCATION: Lancashire
RELATED SUBJECTS: Medical Sciences, Biomedical Sciences
INTERNATIONAL STUDENTS: TBC

Edinburgh

COURSE: A 6 year course which leads to the award of a BSc (Hons) and an MBChB primary medical qualification
The first 2 years are a mixture of science and some clinical experience. Year 3 is an intercalated honours year with a research slant. Years 4-6 will be clinical medicine with specialities.
GRADES: AAA. This must include Chemistry and one other subject from Biology, Mathematics and Physics. Biology is preferred. Only one of Mathematics and Further Mathematics will be considered.
GCSEs: Grade B/6 in Biology, Chemistry, English, Mathematics
ADMISSIONS TEST: UCAT
INTERVIEW: Edinburgh are currently reviewing the potential for interviews. Keep up to date with the website to check this.
LOCATION: Campus university with clinical attachments in surrounding areas
RELATED SUBJECTS: Medical Sciences, Biomedical Sciences
INTERNATIONAL STUDENTS: Accepted

Exeter

COURSE: A 5 year course with an option of a 6 year course to obtain an intercalated degree
The course offers clinical exposure from the first month of studying but more in later years
GRADES: A*AA/AAA Applicants must study A Level Chemistry and Biology
GCSEs: No GCSE requirements stated
ADMISSIONS TEST: UCAT
INTERVIEW: Multiple Mini Interviews
LOCATION: First 2 years will be based on campus and then following years based around the South West
RELATED SUBJECTS: Medical Sciences, Biological Sciences. Biological and Medicinal Chemistry
INTERNATIONAL STUDENTS: Accepted

Glasgow

COURSE: A 5 year course but an option of a longer course with a one-year intercalated BSc degree or a two-year BSc (Hons)
The course offers clinical exposure from the first year but most clinical exposure in later years
GRADES: AAA
Applicants must study A Level Chemistry and one of Maths, Physics or Biology. If Biology is not studied at A level, it must have been taken at AS-level and a Grade A is required
GCSEs: A minimum of grade B/6 in English
ADMISSIONS TEST: UCAT
INTERVIEW: Traditional interview
LOCATION: Three main Campus's with clinical attachments in surrounding area
RELATED SUBJECTS: Human Biology, Anatomy, Nursing
INTERNATIONAL STUDENTS: Accepted

Hull/York

COURSE: A 5 year course with the option of a 6 year course to intercalate to gain a BSc
The course offers clinical exposure in the first year but most clinical exposure in later years
GRADES: AAA
Applicants must study A Level Biology and Chemistry with a pass in practical experiments
GCSEs: A minimum of 8 GCSE's at grade 9-4, or A*-C. A minimum of grade B is required in English Language and Maths
ADMISSIONS TEST: UCAT
INTERVIEW: Multiple Mini Interviews including a 20-minute group assessment to highlight how effectively you work in a team
LOCATION: Two main Campuses with clinical attachments in surrounding areas
RELATED SUBJECTS: Biomedical Sciences
INTERNATIONAL STUDENTS: Accepted

Imperial College

COURSE: A 6 year course which leads to the award of both a BSc and an MBBS qualification
The first 2 years are a mixture of science and starting clinical medicine. Year 3 consists of three 10 week clinical attachments. Year 4 is spent studying for the BSC. Year 5 and 6 consists of studying the specialities in medicine
GRADES: A*AA
Applicants must achieve a minimum of an A/7 in A Level Chemistry and Biology and an A in any third subject but the standard offer often requires an A*/9
GCSEs: No GCSE requirement for this course
ADMISSIONS TEST: BMAT
INTERVIEW: Traditional Interview
LOCATION: Based in South Kensington for location of study, however will have attachments in a variety of hospitals in and out of London
RELATED SUBJECTS: Medical Biosciences, Biological Sciences
INTERNATIONAL STUDENTS: Accepted

Keele

COURSE: A 5 year course with the option of 6 years if you choose to study for an intercalated degree to gain a BSc
The course has clinical exposure from the first year but most clinical exposure in years 3-5
GRADES: A* A A
Applicants must study A Level Chemistry or Biology and a second science (biology, chemistry, physics, maths/statistics) including a pass in the practical section plus a third academic subject
GCSEs: A minimum of 5As/7 including a minimum of grade B/6 in Mathematics, English & Science
ADMISSIONS TEST: UCAT
INTERVIEW: Multiple Mini Interviews
Also applicants will take an additional test which will assess their ability to perform clinically relevant calculations. It is likely a minimum score will be needed in this test.
LOCATION: Campus university with clinical attachments in surrounding area
RELATED SUBJECTS: Biomedical Sciences
INTERNATIONAL STUDENTS: Accepted

King's College, London

COURSE: A 5 year course with the option of 6 years to intercalate to obtain a BSc
The course offers clinical experience from year 2 with more experience in later years
GRADES: A*AA
Applicants must study Chemistry and Biology.
GCSEs: A minimum of grade B/6 in English Language and Mathematics.
ADMISSIONS TEST: UCAT
INTERVIEW: Multiple Mini Interviews
LOCATION: King's is London's most central university, there are four Campuses across London and clinical medicine is taught in three leading
NHS Trusts around London
RELATED SUBJECTS: Biochemistry, Pharmacology, Human Sciences, Biomedical Sciences
INTERNATIONAL STUDENTS: Accepted

Lancaster

COURSE: A 5 year course
The course offers clinical experience from the first year but more in later years
GRADES: AAA plus a further B in an AS Level
AAA-A*AA if no AS Level is offered
Applicants must study A Level Biology and Chemistry
GCSEs: 9 subjects are needed with a minimum score of 15 points from the nine were: A* or A or 7-9 = 2 points
B/6 = 1 point
A minimum of grade B/6 is required in the Sciences, English Language and Mathematics and all other subjects must have a minimum grade of C/5.
ADMISSIONS TEST: BMAT
INTERVIEW: Multiple Mini Interviews
LOCATION: Campus university with attachments in surrounding areas
RELATED SUBJECTS: Biomedical Sciences, Biological Sciences
INTERNATIONAL STUDENTS: Accepted

Leeds

COURSE: A 5 year course with the option of a 6 year course to intercalate for a BSc
The course offers clinical exposure in the first year but most clinical exposure in later years
GRADES: AAA The applicant must study A Level Chemistry or Biology. If Chemistry is not offered then Biology must be offered with either Physics or Mathematics at A Level.
GCSEs: A minimum of 6 grade A*- Bs/ 9-6 in including Chemistry and Biology (or dual science/double science), English Language and Mathematics, dual/double science, or science and additional science, or Chemistry and Biology
ADMISSION TEST: BMAT
INTERVIEW: Multiple Mini Interviews
LOCATION: Campus university with clinical attachments in surrounding areas
RELATED SUBJECTS: Molecular Medicine, Healthcare Sciences
INTERNATIONAL STUDENTS: Accepted

Leicester

COURSE: A 5 year course with the option of a 6 year course with to intercalate gain a BSc
The course offers clinical experience from the first year with more in further years.
GRADES: AAA Applicants including Chemistry and one of; Biology, Physics or Psychology with predicted or achieved grades. IB applicants must offer 36 or more.
GCSEs: A minimum of grade B or 6 in English Language, Maths and two Sciences, including Chemistry and Biology, or Double Science.
ADMISSION TEST: UCAT
INTERVIEW: Multiple Mini Interviews
LOCATION: Campus university with clinical attachments in surrounding areas
RELATED SUBJECTS: Medical Biochemistry, Medical Genetics, Medical Microbiology
INTERNATIONAL STUDENTS: Accepted

Lincoln

COURSE: To start in September 2019. Students can now apply to study for the University of Nottingham's Medicine BMBS degree based in Lincoln, taught by academic staff from both universities.

A 5 year course.

The course offers small amounts of clinical exposure in the first 3 years but more experience in the last 2 years

GRADES: AAA Applicants including Chemistry and Biology at grade A. IB at a 36 offer.

GCSEs: six GCSEs at grade A/7 including Biology and Chemistry, one of either Physics or Maths must also be passed to grade A/7 with the other being grade B/6 and a minimum of grade B/6 in English Language. Double Science requirement is 7,7 and triple science is 7,7,7.

ADMISSION TEST: UCAT

INTERVIEW: Multiple Mini Interviews

LOCATION: Campus university based in Lincoln.

RELATED SUBJECTS: Biochemistry, Biomedical Science

INTERNATIONAL STUDENTS: Accepted

Liverpool

COURSE: A 5 year course with option of 6 years to intercalate

The course offers clinical experience from first year but more in later years

GRADES: AAA Applicants must study A Level Chemistry and Biology

GCSEs: A minimum score of 15 points in nine subjects where A*/A = 2; B = 1 including Sciences, English Language and Mathematics. All of which must be offered a minimum of grade B

ADMISSIONS TEST: UCAT

INTERVIEW: Multiple Mini Interviews

LOCATION: Campus university with clinical attachments in surrounding areas

RELATED SUBJECTS: Biological and Medical Sciences

INTERNATIONAL STUDENTS: Accepted

Manchester

COURSE: A 5 year course with the option of 6 years to intercalate to gain a BSc or Masters

The course offers clinical experience from Year 1 but more exposure in later years

GRADES: AAA

Applicants must study A Level Chemistry and one from Biology, Human Biology, Physics and Mathematics

GCSEs: A minimum of seven subjects at grade C or above, five of which must be at A or A*

English Language, Mathematics and at least two science subjects are required at GCSE minimum grade B. If Dual Award Science or Core and Additional Science are offered, the minimum required is BB.

ADMISSIONS TEST: UCAT

INTERVIEW: Multiple Mini Interviews

LOCATION: The first 2 years will be on the Central Manchester campus with the remaining years in clinical attachments in hospitals in the surrounding area. In Years 3 to 5 of the medical programme, our students are placed at a base teaching hospital, rather than on campus at Manchester.

RELATED SUBJECTS: Biomedical Sciences, Medical Biochemistry

INTERNATIONAL STUDENTS: Accepted

Newcastle

COURSE: A 5 year course with an option of 6 years if you choose to study for an intercalated degree to gain a BSc

The course has clinical exposure from the first year but most clinical exposure in years 3-5

GRADES: AAA

Applicants must study Chemistry and/or Biology at A or AS level including a pass in the practical element. If only one of Biology and/or Chemistry is offered at A or AS level, the other should be offered at GCSE grade A.

ADMISSIONS TEST: UCAT

INTERVIEW: Multiple Mini Interviews

LOCATION: Campus university with clinical attachments in surrounding area

RELATED SUBJECTS: Biomedical Sciences, Biomedical Genetics

INTERNATIONAL STUDENTS: Accepted

Nottingham

COURSE: A 5 year course with the award of BMedSci after a research project in the third year and BM BS after the fifth year

The course offers small amounts of clinical exposure in the first 3 years but more experience in the last 2 years

GRADES: AAA (plus an A or B in a fourth AS if being taken)

Applicants must study A Level Biology (or Human Biology) and Chemistry Grade A at AS level physics can compensate for achieving grade B at GCSE

GCSEs: A minimum of six grade As to include Biology, Chemistry and Physics (or science double award) and minimum of grade B in Mathematics and English language

If grade B was achieved in GCSE Physics an A at AS Level can compensate for this

ADMISSIONS TEST: UCAT

INTERVIEW: Multiple Mini Interviews

LOCATION: Campus university with clinical attachments in surrounding areas

RELATED SUBJECTS: Biochemistry, Biochemistry and Biological Chemistry

INTERNATIONAL STUDENTS: Accepted

Oxford

COURSE: A six year course gaining a BA after three years, however you have to reapply after 3 years to study clinical medicine at Oxford or you can move to a different university to study this.

The first three years are science based and then the next three years are clinical based.

GRADES: A*AA

Applicants must achieve at least a grade A in both A Level Chemistry and at least one of Biology, Physics or Mathematics

GCSEs: There are no formal GCSE requirements, however at least a grade C in the sciences and mathematics is essential. However, to be successful most applicants have A*'s and A's. ADMISSIONS TEST: BMAT

INTERVIEW: Traditional Interview

LOCATION: College system for pre-clinical studies, variety of attachments in different hospitals in surrounding areas for clinical medicine

RELATED SUBJECTS: Biomedical Sciences, Biological Sciences, Human Sciences or Chemistry

INTERNATIONAL STUDENTS: Accepted

Plymouth

COURSE: A 5 year course with an option of a 6 year course with an intercalated degree to gain a BSc
The course offers clinical exposure in the first year but most clinical exposure in later years
GRADES: A*AA/AAA
Applicants must have a minimum of an A at A Level in both Chemistry and Biology
GCSEs: 7 GCSE's at a minimum of grades A-C/ 9-4 including English language, Mathematics and the Sciences
ADMISSIONS TEST: UCAT
INTERVIEW: Traditional Interview
LOCATION: Campus university with clinical attachments in surrounding areas
RELATED SUBJECTS: Healthcare Sciences, Biological Sciences
INTERNATIONAL STUDENTS: Accepted

Queen Mary, London

COURSE: A 5 year course but with an option of 6 years if you choose to study for an intercalated degree to gain a BSc
The course has clinical exposure from the first term with more clinical exposure in later years
GRADES: A*AA
Applicants must study A Level Chemistry or Biology, plus a third Science or Maths
GCSEs: A minimum of grades AAABBB in any order to include Biology (or Human Biology), Chemistry, English Language, and Mathematics (or Additional Mathematics or Statistics)
ADMISSIONS TEST: UCAT
INTERVIEW: Traditional Interview with a section on a case scenario or topical issue which the candidate will be sent and be able prepare beforehand. It will be a discussion with no 'right' or 'wrong' answers
LOCATION: Campus university with 5 sites across east and central London with clinical attachments in surrounding areas
RELATED SUBJECTS: Biomedical Sciences, Medical Genetics
INTERNATIONAL STUDENTS: Accepted

Queen's, Belfast

COURSE: A 5 year course with option of 6 years to intercalate to gain a BSc
The course offers clinical experience from year 1 with more experience in later years

GRADES: AAA plus A in a fourth AS-level subject
Applicants must study A-level Chemistry plus at least one other A-level from Biology/Human Biology, Mathematics or Physics. If not continued to A Level Biology must be offered at grade A as a fourth AS level or grade B as a fifth AS Level.

GCSEs: A minimum of grade C in Mathematics and C in Physics or CC in Double Award Science if physics is not offered at a higher level. The applicants GCSE scores in the best 9 subjects will be scored with 4 points awarded for an A* and 3 for an A and this will be used to determine interviews.

ADMISSIONS TEST: UCAT

INTERVIEW: Multiple Mini Interviews

LOCATION: Campus university with clinical attachments in surrounding areas

RELATED SUBJECTS: Biomedical Sciences

INTERNATIONAL STUDENTS: Accepted

Sheffield

COURSE: A 5 year course with the option of a 6 year course to intercalate.
The course offers clinical experience from first year with more as the course progresses

GRADES: AAA
Applicants must study A Level Chemistry and one other science including Maths, Physics, Biology or Psychology with a pass in the practical component. The combination of Chemistry and Biology is acceptable

GCSEs: A minimum of 5 grade A/7 GCSE subjects. GCSE passes at grade B/6 or above in Mathematics, English and at least one science subject (which may be dual awards).

ADMISSION TEST: UCAT

INTERVIEW: Multiple Mini Interviews, including a station where there will be discussion of the Situational Judgement Test from the UCAT

LOCATION: Campus university with clinical attachments in surrounding areas

RELATED SUBJECTS: Biomedical Sciences

INTERNATIONAL STUDENTS: Accepted

Southampton

COURSE: A 5 year course with an option of 6 years to intercalate to achieve a masters in a Medical Science degree
The course offers clinical exposure in the first few weeks but more in later years
GRADES: AAA Applicants must study A Level Chemistry and Biology
GCSEs: A minimum of 6 GCSEs at grade A/7 or above, including either Maths, Biology and Chemistry, or Maths, additional science and science. English language is required at a minimum of grade B/6.
including Mathematics, English
Language and Sciences
ADMISSION TEST: UCAT
INTERVIEW: Selection Days – no other information available
LOCATION: Campus university with clinical attachments in surrounding areas
RELATED SUBJECTS: Biomedical Sciences
INTERNATIONAL STUDENTS: Accepted

St Andrews

COURSE: A 6 year course with the first 3 years based in St Andrews to gain a BSc Honours. You then will proceed to clinical training at one of the five partner Medical Schools including the University of Aberdeen, Dundee, Edinburgh, Glasgow and Manchester, where an MBChB degree will be gained.
Small amounts of clinical exposure in first few years
GRADES: AAA including Chemistry and one other of Biology, Mathematics or Physics
If Biology, Mathematics and English are not offered at A2 or AS Level, each must normally have been passed at GCSE grade B or better. Dual award Science is not acceptable in lieu of GCSE Biology.
GCSEs: A minimum of 5 A/7 grades, those with achieved Advanced Levels, may be considered with less than five A grades.
ADMISSION TEST: UCAT
INTERVIEW: Multiple Mini Interviews
In addition, the university use the Situational Judgement Test (SJT) from the UCAT as part of the interview process with the score being incorporated into the final interview score
LOCATION: Campus university with clinical attachments in surrounding area of partner Medical Schools
RELATED SUBJECTS: Biology and Psychology, Biochemistry
INTERNATIONAL STUDENTS: Accepted

St George's, London

COURSE: A 5 years with option of 6 years to intercalate
The course offers clinical experience from the first year but more in later years. A 4 year course is available for Graduate applicants.
GRADES: AAA
Applicants must study A Level include Chemistry and Biology/Human Biology
GCSEs: A minimum requirement 5 GCSE grades at grade A/6 or above. This must include English Language, Mathematics and Science (Double or Triple Science award).
ADMISSIONS TEST: UCAT
INTERVIEW: Multiple Mini Interviews
LOCATION: Campus university with clinical attachments in surrounding areas
RELATED SUBJECTS: Biomedical Science, Paramedic Science
INTERNATIONAL STUDENTS: Accepted

Sunderland

COURSE: Starts in 2019. A 5 year course.
The course offers clinical experience from first year with more as the course progresses
GRADES: A Levels in three subjects at grades of AAA are required, including Biology or Chemistry plus another designated science subject (Biology, Chemistry, Physics, Maths/Further Maths/Statistics) and a third academic subject.
GCSEs: A minimum of 5 grade A/7 GCSE subjects. GCSE passes at grade B/6 or above in Mathematics, English, Biology, Chemistry and Physics..
ADMISSION TEST: UCAT
INTERVIEW: Multiple Mini Interviews.
LOCATION: New building and facilities- all non clinical parts of the course provided here
RELATED SUBJECTS: Adult Nursing, Public Health
INTERNATIONAL STUDENTS: Not Accepted

University College London

COURSE: A 6 year course which leads to the award of both a BSc and a medical degree
The course has clinical experience from the first year with more clinical medicine in later years
GRADES: A*AA
Applicants must study A Level Chemistry and Biology with the A* grade being in one of these subjects
GCSEs: A minimum of grade B in both English Language and Mathematics. Also minimum of GSCE grade C in a modern foreign language (excluding Ancient Greek, Biblical Hebrew or Latin)
If an applicant cannot offer a foreign language, they can still be accepted into the university but would be obliged to take a language course during their first year
ADMISSIONS TEST: BMAT
INTERVIEW: Traditional Interview with potential discussion of BMAT essay
LOCATION: Three main campuses in London with clinical attachments in surrounding areas
RELATED SUBJECTS: Applied Medical Sciences, Nutrition and Medical Sciences
INTERNATIONAL STUDENTS: Accepted

In addition to the universities listed which offer traditional undergraduate Medicine courses, three courses in the UK have more specialised offerings. For more information on these, please visit the universities' websites.

University of Central Lancashire

This university offers a Medicine course specifically for non-EU students. A limited number of places will be available for UK students from the North West of England. Weighting will be given to UK Widening Participation students.

University of Warwick

This university offers the UK's largest graduate-entry only Medicine programme.

Swansea University

This university offers a graduate-entry only Medicine programme.

4 THE PERSONAL STATEMENT

The Personal Statement

For any university course you apply to, the Personal Statement allows you to demonstrate your academic capabilities and convey your interest in the subject, as well as showing why you are a suitable applicant. For Medicine, however, a fantastic Personal Statement is essential due to the extremely high competition for places.

In this chapter, we explain the purpose of the Personal Statement and how it can influence your application. We also provide a guide to planning, writing and proofing which will help you to begin the process of putting together an excellent statement.

WHEN BEGINNING TO WRITE YOUR STATEMENT, YOU SHOULD CONSIDER THE FOLLOWING QUESTIONS:

How important is the Personal Statement?
A strong application for Medicine to any UK university requires you to excel at every stage of the process – including your Personal Statement. Although a strong Personal Statement is not enough to secure a place on its own, it can go a long way towards a successful application, and is definitely necessary for success. The statement can help you at interview, as it discloses your intellectual and medical interests to Admissions Tutors, which in some cases will form part of the interview discussion in both traditional and MMI interviews.

How is the statement used at interview?
You should view everything you say in your Personal Statement as a potential springboard for discussion at interview. You may be asked to elaborate on something you have written about, be it a book, work experience, particular areas of academic interest, or an extended project. With many universities using the MMI format, it is not uncommon for a whole station (i.e. a section of the assessment) to be based on your Personal Statement.

A previous candidate for Medicine at Oxbridge stated: "We discussed action potentials, haemoglobin, cardiac output, respiratory systems, hormones, the liver, mental health… nothing was asked out of the blue – it all led from what I had said in my Personal Statement, or stemmed from a graph."

Even if you are not overtly asked about your Personal Statement at interview, the preparation that goes into researching and writing it will give you the knowledge and confidence to talk about and explore new ideas within your subject, which will only help to make your application stronger.

How can I write a statement when applying for different subjects?
You can only submit one Personal Statement through UCAS, so it will be read by Admissions Tutors at all the universities you apply to. Applicants for Medicine can apply for a maximum of four Medicine courses, but also have the option of applying for a fifth non-Medicine course.

The Personal Statement needs to show your dedication and commitment to Medicine, but at the same time you can also ensure it has some relevance to your fifth-choice course. For example, if you choose to apply for Pharmacy as your fifth choice, you can include a sentence on drugs and medicine.

Should I include extra-curricular activities in my Personal Statement?

It is important to consider how much content you include not relating directly to the medical course you are applying for. Oxford and Cambridge, for instance, are not particularly interested in whether you are a gifted athlete or play instruments to Grade 8 standard. They do, of course, recognise the scale of such accomplishments, and they can indicate characteristics that will boost academic success. Ultimately, however, the Admissions Tutors reading your statement care about one thing: how much potential do you have as a medical student? Other universities are often more interested in students as 'well-rounded' people, where your extracurricular activities are of value. As such, it is a good idea to include these, but make sure to state how these extracurricular activities will help you to become an excellent medical student and doctor.

If you are applying to Oxbridge, you must strongly weight your statement towards subject-specific content. The guide later in this chapter shows how you can do this.

Can I submit more than one Personal Statement?

While you can only submit one Personal Statement through UCAS and the universities you apply to, there is one exception. Applicants to Durham have the option of submitting a 'substitute Personal Statement', which allows you to submit a separate Personal Statement to Durham directly following your UCAS application.

If you choose to do so, the Admissions Tutors at Durham will then disregard your UCAS Personal Statement and only read the submitted substitute statement. This substitute has exactly the same requirements as the normal statement (i.e. 4000 characters) and must be submitted within 3 days of receiving Durham's email acknowledging their receipt of your application.

What is the SAQ?

For Cambridge applicants, the Supplementary Application Questionnaire (SAQ) provides you with the opportunity to elaborate on your motivation for applying to your chosen course, as well as further information about your grades. One part of the SAQ, for example, requires you to submit your individual module marks in AS and/or A Levels.

As part of the SAQ, you have the opportunity to write an additional statement, which Admissions Tutors consider in addition to your UCAS Personal Statement. This is your chance to mention anything you have not been able to include in your UCAS Personal Statement, including further reading or more detail on your extended essay or EPQ.

The SAQ must be completed by all UK and EU applicants by the deadline of 22nd October (one week after the 15th October UCAS deadline). You will receive an email with the details you need to complete the SAQ form once you have submitted your UCAS form. If you are submitting a COPA you will not need to fill in the entirety of the SAQ, but will need to complete your UCAS ID number and COPA Reference Number to submit.

WRITING YOUR PERSONAL STATEMENT

This section explains how you can begin the process of writing your statement using advice from the book 60 Successful Personal Statements For UCAS application – co-written by Guy Nobes, Head of Guidance at Marlborough College, and Gavin Nobes, Senior Lecturer at the University of East Anglia.

Staring at a blank page and no idea where to begin? Try the steps below...

Step 1: Structure and planning

1. Take a piece of A4 paper and draw a line across it about three inches from the top. Do the same three inches from the bottom.

2. Start with the bottom third. Bullet-point all the extracurricular achievements you can think of. Good at piano? Put it in. Climbed Mount Kilimanjaro? Put it in. Played Polonius in the school play? DofE gold medal? Sure, why not? You don't need to hold back or edit the list yet: this is just the planning stage.

3. Now the top third. The opening sentence is often the hardest, but a good way to begin is to take 15-20 minutes to think seriously about the real reason you're choosing your degree. Try not to feel embarrassed about clichés at this stage. This is the plan: you can make it sound sophisticated later. Strong Personal Statements begin with a real sentiment, rather than something you think the Admissions Tutors will want to hear. The question 'Why do you want to study X?' is almost guaranteed at some point in the interview. Don't disregard it: this is probably the single most important element of your application. A good answer should demonstrate a real understanding of what the academic discipline of your subject is all about, as well as your motivation for pursuing it.

4. Now the middle. Your middle section is your content. What work experience have you carried out? What did you learn and how will you use this during your medical studies? What voluntary work have you participated in? Again: what has this taught you that will help make you a great doctor? What extra work have you done that has best demonstrated your dedication to medicine? This section is to

show work you have done outside your A Level (or IB or equivalent) syllabus – and your devotion to medicine.

To help focus your ideas and get your creative juices flowing, try jotting down some answers to the following questions on a separate sheet. Remember, this is all about your subject, so keep it relevant:

- What have you read and/or done to help further your understanding of the Medicine course at your chosen university?

- How do you think your current academic subjects will support your chosen course and help you to excel at university?

- What part of your current studies has most inspired you and why?

- What books or articles have you recently read?

- What did you enjoy about them? What do you feel you learned from reading them? (Think about what challenged you or whether anything surprised you.) Did you agree or disagree with the author/s? Did the particular book/article make you want to learn more about a certain subject? If so, what exactly? How might they relate to medicine?

- What work experience have you done that is relevant to medicine?

Once you've got these, select the strongest points and bullet-point them in your middle section. It's a good idea to start making a list of all of relevant activities or books as soon as you have decided to apply for Medicine – this ensures early on that you will have something interesting to write about.

Your Personal Statement should mention texts and articles that you feel comfortable with. Everyone will tell you to be sure to read those texts, but it is also useful to think of them as doorways to a network of further wider reading that you've looked into. This is why it is key to have more material ready than is in your 4000 characters.

Check out the bibliography and references in the book that you mention in your Personal Statement, and read some of the journals/articles mentioned. When you go into your interview, you will have a wealth of material to draw from so that you are not caught short when trying to answer a question using an example.

Step 2: Refining and writing

1. Bottom third: reassess your extracurriculars. Could any of them have furthered your understanding of your subject? Select two or three stand-out achievements and find elements of them that could contribute to your being good in the subject. Perhaps you ran a marathon? Tenacity, physical and mental stamina will be invaluable for a career as a doctor.
2. Look at your bulleted content for the middle section again. What was it about each experience that highlighted to you how special your subject is? Once you have considered this, look at how you might draw thematic links between each experience in order to lead logically from one idea to the next.
3. It's a good general rule of thumb to approach your subject and what interests you about it from three different angles across three successive paragraphs.

Step 3: Checking your tone

When you are planning and writing your statement, it is vital to be aware that bad Personal Statements try to make a mini-essay out of each subject mentioned, in order to try to demonstrate knowledge of the text or idea. There is not enough space to develop a complex idea – save that for your interview! When you write your Personal Statement, isolate a particular reason that you have taken an interest in medicine and engaged with it, and then use specific examples to back up this general idea.

When writing, you can assume a certain level of knowledge on the part of the reader: you do not have to explain what the Duke of Edinburgh Award scheme is, for example. This applies, more importantly, to books you are writing about. You don't need to describe what a book is about – rather, write about what you think of it and what the argument means to you. Be specific and give examples to show that you have actually read the book and have formulated an opinion.

TEN GOLDEN RULES

It's a good idea to review your statement in light of the following guidelines – this will help you to produce your best writing.

1. Research the courses you are applying for thoroughly – to show enthusiasm for and understanding of the subject.
2. Be specific and display precise knowledge: never be vague.
3. Be honest – only include what you know and are confident about discussing.
4. Try to sound interesting and interested, but don't overdo it, gush or come across as arrogant.
5. Express your information and ideas clearly.
6. Don't be negative: try to see any failures as 'learning experiences'.
7. Organise your material clearly and logically.
8. Don't state the obvious or repeat yourself.
9. Check spelling, use of apostrophes and grammar thoroughly: mistakes are irritating to read and don't reflect well on you!
10. Don't misuse words in an attempt to look clever – your Personal Statement needs to be clear as well as reflecting the way you communicate.

"Although aware of its negative aspects and limitations, I still believe medicine is the ideal career for me. Becoming a doctor would allow me to help others in a job combining my strong interest in science, enjoyment of communicating with others, and working within a team – as well as varied future opportunities such as teaching and research. As a keen, diligent, and determined individual capable of working well under pressure, I feel I will be prepared for the demands of the course and the career."

An applicant for Medicine at Cambridge

THE PLATINUM RULE

The best all-purpose rule for success is: Show – don't tell! Rather than just claiming to be enthusiastic or informed about your subject, demonstrate your interest and understanding by describing:
The background to your interest in the subject
*   Ways in which you are currently following up this enthusiasm
*   What exactly you know about the subject

Remember: while the Personal Statement can take a good deal of your time, do keep reminding yourself that this is the chance to write on a very interesting subject that no one else will be writing about: you!

5 GRADUATE ENTRY MEDICINE

Graduate Entry Medicine

Applying for Medicine as your undergraduate degree is not your only opportunity to pursue a career as a doctor. The Graduate Entry Medicine (GEM) course provides another route into the profession for graduates from different degrees – both for those with science backgrounds and those without. While some graduates may take another undergraduate degree in Medicine, the GEM allows graduates to take an accelerated programme, consisting of fewer (but more intensive) years of study. As with the undergraduate course, GEM is known for its competitive application process and intense and challenging content.

While many aspects of the graduate Medicine application process are similar to the process for undergraduate courses, there are differences to be aware of. This chapter will guide you through the Graduate Entry Medicine course and the application process, including tips from current graduate medical students.

SELECTING YOUR MEDICAL SCHOOL

Not all medical schools offer graduate entry courses, so you need to ensure that you do your research. While all medical schools will ensure that you leave as a competent junior doctor, there are variations in size, location and course structure. You will be spending a minimum of four years at your chosen university, so it is important that it's the right fit. For example, do you have a preference for a city-based medical school like Queen Mary's London or a campus-based school such as Warwick? As of 2019, there are 15 universities which offer the accelerated GEM course. These are Birmingham, Cambridge, Cardiff, Dundee/St Andrews Imperial, King's College London, Liverpool, Newcastle, Nottingham, Oxford, Queen Mary's London, Southampton, St George's London, Swansea and Warwick.

AM I ELIGIBLE?

The type of undergraduate degree that you've completed will have a direct impact on your eligibility for each course. As a general rule, all courses are open to science graduates, although the definition of 'science' may differ. If you have completed an arts degree, your options are more limited. Of all universities that run GEM courses, only seven accept candidates from non-science undergraduate courses. These universities are Cambridge, Newcastle, Nottingham, Southampton, St George's London, Swansea and Warwick. Even candidates from non-science backgrounds will in many cases be expected to have taken Chemistry at A Level, so check the individual course requirements for your chosen university.

Outside of these restrictions, students often worry that certain subjects will be looked upon more favourably than others. While it is true that your undergraduate university and course may be a contributing factor in whether you are invited to interview, the graduate entry Medicine course is intrinsically inclusive. It is designed to allow those who have decided on a career in Medicine later in life, as well as those from a 'non-traditional' background to access the profession.

Most Admissions Tutors keep this at the forefront of their mind, which means that greater weight is generally placed on Admissions Tests, interviews and your personal motivations, rather than just your undergraduate degree. However, it is important to be aware that whatever course you studied or university you went to, you will in most cases need to have achieved a 2:1 or have a further postgraduate degree to be eligible for entry.

WHAT IS THE ADMISSIONS PROCESS?
As with the undergraduate Medicine courses, the application varies between universities. For instance, King's College London is known to place a large emphasis on the UCAT score when considering applicants, whereas the University of Cambridge does not require applicants to sit the UCAT at all. It is advisable to do your research into the different admissions processes and consider which will allow you to play to your strengths.

HOW IS THE COURSE STRUCTURED?
As with undergraduate degree courses, the GEM courses are not all identical. Some universities, such as Warwick, offer purely graduate courses, while others integrate graduates with undergraduates early on. Similarly, some universities, such as Oxford and Cambridge, have a

more academic focus, and thus may suit those interested in a career in medical research.

THE APPLICATION

Much of the graduate application process is similar to that for undergraduate applications. The focus of this chapter is to provide additional information that is important for graduate Medicine applicants, but ensure you read the relevant chapters on each stage of the process for a complete understanding of the process.

THE PERSONAL STATEMENT

The personal statement provides an opportunity for you to impress Admissions Tutors with your relevant achievements prior to medical school, and more importantly, to demonstrate the motivation for your application. The competitive nature of the graduate entry course, along with the hugely diverse range of applications, means that the personal statement is a significant part of the application – perhaps even more so than for the undergraduate course. Your personal statement should at the very least address two key areas:

YOUR PERSONAL REASONS FOR WANTING TO APPLY TO MEDICINE

It is essential to address your reasons for applying for the Medicine course. It might be that you've always wanted to read Medicine but never felt it was achievable, or that an experience of an ill family member drew you to the profession. Whatever the reason, it should be clear and honest – remember that the Admissions Tutors will have seen hundreds of personal statements and can tell when a student is not being straightforward. The essence of the personal statement should be about you as an individual, and the best way to achieve this is by using your reason for applying for Medicine as the framework to build upon.

YOUR WORK EXPERIENCE

When you apply for Medicine, you are not just applying to a degree course, but a vocation. Admissions Tutors are looking for students who are aware of the challenges and responsibilities involved in the medical profession, and your personal statement is the place to demonstrate that you have a full appreciation of what the career entails. Graduate entry applicants will often be facing a significant opportunity cost, both

in terms of time and money, and getting a range of work experience will allow you to truly decide whether Medicine is the right path for you. Demonstrating that you have taken the time to experience and understand what it is like to be a doctor will prove to Admissions Tutors that you are aware and committed to undertaking a Medicine degree.
Referencing work experience in your personal statement also gives you an opportunity to show that you have developed certain core skills that are crucial for any doctor, such as empathy, teamwork and communication skills. These skills will often be tested in interview, but your personal statement is your first chance to demonstrate your suitability for becoming a doctor.

Most universities will not even consider an applicant without work experience, and certain universities require that applicants complete a certain number of weeks, so ensure you do your research before applying and demonstrate the necessary written work in your personal statement.

GETTING WORK EXPERIENCE AND MAKING THE MOST OF IT
Throughout the application, graduate entry applicants will be held to a higher degree of expectation concerning both the amount and quality of work experience undertaken. Securing work experience can be challenging so it is best to approach it from several angles. Some applicants try personal contacts or their local GP, and many hospitals are beginning to open up work experience schemes. However, universities do recognise that securing hospital work can be difficult, so will accept non-hospital based work experience. Consider volunteering opportunities at a local hospice, care home, or organisations such as St John's Ambulance or the Red Cross.

Far more important than where you do your work experience is what you gain from it. Take the opportunity to improve your understanding of the experience and challenges faced by not only doctors, but by patients and healthcare professionals – ensure that you ask questions and reflect on what you observe.

ADMISSIONS TESTS
Universities may require you to sit one of three exams: the UCAT, BMAT or GAMSAT. You can find out more about the UCAT and BMAT in Chapter

4, but bear in mind that as a graduate applicant you will be expected to achieve higher marks than undergraduate applicants.

The Graduate Medical School Admissions Test (GAMSAT) is designed to evaluate your suitability for the course and is composed of three sections: reasoning in humanities and social sciences, written communication, and reasoning in biological and physical sciences. This final section is equivalent to equivalent to first-year university level chemistry and biology, and A Level physics.

The test itself will take an entire day to complete and can only be sat on one specific date.

The table below outlines the format of the exam.

Section	Number of questions	Reading time in minute	Writing time in minutes
Section I, Reasoning in Humanities	75	10	100
Section II, Written Communication	2	5	60
Section III, Reasoning in Biological and Physical Sciences	110	10	170

For more information and material, visit the GAMSAT website (https://gamsat.acer.edu.au/)

THE INTERVIEW

Many students find the interview the most daunting part of the application process. Although it can seem intimidating, the interview is an opportunity to demonstrate your ability and prove you are capable of being an excellent doctor.

The style of interview for graduate entry courses vary greatly across universities, so make sure to take the time to familiarize yourself with the interview format of your chosen universities. The most popular structure is the Multiple Mini Interview or MMI process, where you will visit different stations, taking on a variety of tasks which could include a traditional interview, taking a patient's medical history, or even team tasks. These interviews are assessing key skills needed to be a doctor, such as empathy and communication. However, this isn't the only format; some universities conduct traditional academic interviews, or incorporate specific aspects such as a discussion of the BMAT essay.

TIPS FOR APPROACHING YOUR INTERVIEW

1. Make sure you have a framework for answers to typical interview style questions, such as 'why Medicine?', 'tell me about your work experience' or 'do you understand the realities of life as a doctor?'

2. Ensure you are aware of current affairs, changes and advances surrounding the medical profession. The best way to do this is to keep up-to-date consistently throughout the application, by reading healthcare journals such as the BMJ and the New Scientist, the NHS website, and generally staying aware of the news. Consider questions surrounding current issues; for example, you may be asked to speak about a medical development you've read about, or your opinion on the Junior Doctor strike.

3. Consider how you would answer ethics-based questions. The purpose of these questions is to assess what you have read around medical ethics and whether you are able to apply what you have read to a particular scenario. They can be difficult questions to answer because there is often no 'right' answer and it can be difficult not to get tangled up in possibilities rather than answer directly. The best way to prepare is to look at past ethics questions and discuss the problems with a friend or family member.

4. The level of scientific knowledge you will be tested on varies across universities, but it is vital for you to have a basic understanding of key diseases and how they affect individuals, good examples of which are heart disease and diabetes. If you know the course is particularly science-based, it is also a good idea to ensure you

have a solid knowledge of biology and chemistry so that you can face challenging questions which draw on your undergraduate knowledge. Make sure you do your research about the courses you've applied for, as this will help to guide your preparation in this area.

As with undergraduate Medicine courses, Graduate Entry Medicine is a competitive course, with many students vying for the chance to succeed as a medical professional. Understanding the admissions process outlined in this chapter is a useful starting point to help you begin to compile a competitive application for the GEM course, and hopefully the beginnings of your career as a doctor.

6 ADMISSIONS TESTS

Admission Test

This chapter will inform you about the main admissions tests universities will ask you sit, and show you how to prepare for each one – including example questions for you to try.

WHICH COURSES REQUIRE WHICH TEST?

- The following institutions require the BioMedical Admissions Test (BMAT):
    - Undergraduate Medicine at Cambridge, Oxford, UCL, Imperial, Brighton & Sussex, Keele, Lancaster, Leeds, and Lee Kong Chian (Singapore).
    - Graduate Medicine at Imperial and Oxford.
    - Biomedical Sciences at Oxford.
    - Veterinary Medicine at Cambridge. – Dentistry at Leeds.

- The following institutions require the University Clinical Aptitude Test (UCAT):
    - Undergraduate Medicine at Aberdeen, Birmingham, Bristol, Cardiff, East Anglia, Edinburgh, Exeter, Glasgow, Hull York Medical School, Keele, KCL, Leicester, Liverpool, Manchester, Newcastle, Nottingham, Plymouth, Queen Mary, Queens Belfast, Sheffield, Southampton, St Andrew's, and St George's.
    - Graduate Medicine at KCL, Warwick, Newcastle, Queen Mary, and Southampton.
    - Dentistry at Aberdeen, Liverpool, Bristol, Birmingham, Dundee, Glasgow, KCL, Liverpool, Queen Mary, Sheffield, and Queen's Belfast.

- The following institutions require the Graduate Australian Medical School Admissions Test (GAMSAT):
    - Graduate Medicine at Nottingham, Cardiff, Swansea, Liverpool, Exeter, Plymouth, and St George's.
    - Graduate Dentistry at Plymouth.

WHY ARE THE ADMISSIONS TESTS IMPORTANT?

Applicants to medical school are often the brightest and most dedicated students, and as a result they will often have similar grade profiles.

This, along with the recent A Level reforms, make the Admissions Tests an important part of the application process. Admissions Tests are another element of the application process that allows the universities to differentiate between candidates. For some universities, your performance can determine whether or not you will be invited to interview. The Admissions Tests are partly designed to 'level the playing field', with applicants across the world sitting the same test under exam conditions. You should think of these tests as another opportunity for you to prove your suitability for and dedication to medicine.

SHOULD I PREPARE?

Whichever type of test you are taking, you are likely to perform much better if you understand it before you sit it. Some aspects of the tests are similar to IQ test questions and do not require specific subject knowledge, and the biggest challenge of these exams is time pressure. The best way to prepare is to read our tips for approaching the tests below and then get started with some practise questions.

Top tips for preparing
Know the structure, format and mark scheme
Knowing how the test works will enable you to work on your exam technique in the most efficient way. Think about your strengths and weaknesses in relation to the test and how you can improve on these. Plan your approach to the test, particularly taking into account the timing and structure of each section. Familiarity with the structure will help you to relax during the test itself. You should also find out out how many marks the different sections of the test carry, so that you can allocate the right amount of time to each section. This will help you maximise your score and avoid running out of time before you reach the final question.

Practise, practise, practise
The most efficient and successful way for you to prepare is to do practise papers. By practicing past papers, you improve your ability to apply your knowledge and skills within the time limit. This method also allows you to review the answers you get wrong, consider how you might have approached the question differently, and decide what particular skills you need to work on. Practise your mental maths – for example, times tables and how to quickly work out fractions, percentages and decimals.

Top Tips when taking the test

1. ANSWER EVERY QUESTION
2. Don't panic – if you're struggling and getting nowhere with a question, make an educated guess and move on
3. Eliminate obviously wrong answers where possible: this makes guesses more successful
4. Ensure good exam conditions: if you're feeling unwell on the day, reschedule the test (where possible), and ask for earplugs if you are disturbed by others leaving/arriving
5. Keep an eye on the clock
6. Sketch or draw out information when relevant
7. Where indicated, forget prior knowledge and just use what the test is giving you
8. READ THE QUESTION CAREFULLY
9. Remember the 'CATSPINE' mnemonic for abstract reasoning – Colour, Angles, Type, Shape, Position, Intersections, Number and Edges.

Our next section goes into detail on each of the Admissions Tests, with advice from our graduate tutors on what type of preparation really makes a difference, and help with approaching example questions. Always check the individual test and university websites for all the latest updates, including dates, timings, deadlines, marking and the structure of the tests. More resources can also be found on the Admissions Testing Service and the Oxbridge Applications website (www.oxbridgeapplications.com).
Good luck!

BioMedical Admissions Test (BMAT)

The BMAT test is two hours long and consists of three sections – one on Aptitude and Skills (similar in style to an IQ test), one on Scientific Knowledge and Applications, and finally a Writing Task. While views on the difficulty of tests are subjective, the BMAT is commonly thought to be harder and more varied than the UCAT test.

When: Registration for the exam takes place in September and October with your chosen test centre. The BMAT is sat on the first Wednesday in November worldwide.

Where: You can sit the test at any centre that administers the BMAT, including many schools and colleges. If your school is not a BMAT centre, then you can take it at another local authorised test centre.

Cost: It costs £45 to take the exam within the EU; overseas applicants are asked to pay £76. An additional £32 is added if registration is made late. There is some support for those who would find it difficult to pay – check the website.

Results: Your universities will find out your result in mid-late November, and can make a decision on whether to offer an interview at that point. You will find out your score soon after and can appeal it for a fee.

COMPOSITION OF THE BMAT

The BMAT is split into 3 sections:

Section 1 – Aptitude and Skills
This section is similar to an IQ test, with varied questions testing skills such as problem-solving, comprehension of arguments, data analysis and logical inference. You need to be competent at rapid mental mathematics and reasoning skills, and be able to check your answers as you go along. There are 35 multiple-choice questions (MCQs) to answer in 60 minutes.

Section 2 – Scientific Knowledge and Applications
This section tests your understanding of basic science and maths, using knowledge that most people will have covered in GCSE/iGCSE Biology, Chemistry, Physics and Maths. It can draw on topics such as genetics, electricity, or how the pH of blood changes. There are 27 MCQs to complete in 30 minutes.

Section 3 – Writing Task
This section asks you to write an essay, testing your ability to select, develop and structure a logical argument, back it up with evidence, and communicate concisely and effectively. You are given a choice of four questions (one is tailored towards veterinary students) and asked to write one essay in 30 minutes. The question will indicate how you should approach the answer, essentially giving you the structure your essay should take. Because space is limited to one A4 side, we also strongly advise you to spend the first ten minutes selecting and planning your essay from the options – this means you'll be able to make the most of the time and space available over the whole 30 minutes.

SCORING

Sections 1 & 2
The scores of sections 1 and 2 are individually standardised and fitted around a bell curve. Each question is worth 1 point, and these marks from the whole cohort are compiled onto a bell curve. This curve runs from minimum 1.0 to maximum 9.0, and the average BMAT candidate therefore scores around 5.0. The most competitive candidates will be scoring above 6.0, and the best can get 7.0 upwards.

Section 3
Two examiners will mark your essay and grade it on two criteria – you will receive a letter for the quality of your written English, and a number for the quality of your content.
These two scores are combined to give an average – i.e. if one examiner awards you a 3A, and the other a 4C, you will overall receive a 3.5B. The best score is 5A and the worst 1E: most good applicants should receive at least a 3A.

HOW DO UNIVERSITIES USE THE BMAT?

These scores are used differently by the various universities, with some placing emphasis on high performance overall, and others focusing more on success in the science or essay sections.

EXAMPLE QUESTIONS

Section 1

1a) A car averages a speed of 30mph over a certain distance and then returns over the same distance at an average speed of 20mph. What is the average speed for the journey?

       A. 22.5 mph
       B. 24 mph
       C. 25 mph
       D. 26 mph
       E. 27.5 mph
       F The distance travelled is required to calculate average speed.

1b) All Staphylococci are bacteria and all bacteria are Prokaryotes. No Staphylococci are Archaea. Which of the following must be true?

       A.   Some bacteria are Archaea.
       B.   Staphylococci are not Prokaryotes.
       C.   All Prokaryotes are Archaea.
       D.   All Archaea are Prokaryotes.
       E.   Some Staphylococci are not bacteria.
       F.   None of the above.

Section 2

2a) Calculate the number of planets in the universe that could harbour life if there are 200 billion galaxies in the observable universe; each galaxy has 300,000 million stars; each star has 8 planets; and the probability of life developing on any given planet is 0.01%.

       A. 48×10^{16}
       B. 48×10^{17}
       C. 48×10^{18}
       D. 48×10^{19}
       E. 48×10^{20}
       F. 48×10^{21}

2b) Some breathalysers use potassium dichromate crystals and ethanol. In the reaction, the orange dichromate ion $Cr_2O_7{}^{2-}$, changes to the green chromium ion Cr^{3+}. Which of the following statements is true?

A. Chromium has lost electrons and its oxidation state has decreased.

B. Chromium has lost electrons and its oxidation state has increased.

C. Chromium has gained electrons and its oxidation state has decreased.

D. Chromium has gained electrons and its oxidation state has increased.

E. More information is required to calculate the change in oxidation state.

Section 3

3a) "Man cannot discover new oceans unless he has the courage to lose sight of the shore."

André Gide

Explain what this statement means. Argue to the contrary that discovery can be made whilst not "losing sight of the shore". To what extent, if any, do you think Gide is correct?

3 b) "Medicine is an art; not a science."

Explain what this statement means. Argue to the contrary that medicine is in fact a science, using examples to illustrate your answer. To what extent, if any, is medicine an art?

For the answers to all the above questions, as well as advice on how to approach them, visit www.dukesmedicalapplications.com. We have up-to-date information on the test dates and deadlines, as well as more detailed information on how your BMAT score will be used in your application.

University Clinical Aptitude Test (UCAT)

The UCAT exam is taken by students applying for Medicine, Dentistry and Biomedical Sciences. Rather than testing scientific knowledge, it examines candidates' cognitive abilities and clinical aptitude.

There are five sections to the exam: verbal reasoning, quantitative reasoning, abstract reasoning, a situational judgment test, and decisionmaking. The UCAT exam is commonly held to be more like an IQ test than a conventional written examination.

When: Deadline for registration is mid-September, and you may sit the test any time between July and the end of September. Unlike the BMAT, it is your choice when to sit the UCAT. The final date is usually at the beginning of October. You are advised to prepare for the test over the summer, and sit it in early-mid September before you apply to universities via UCAS – it can help determine which universities are appropriate for you.

Where: You can sit the UCAT at any registered centre worldwide – generally in the UK this is a Pearson Vue Test Centre (the same place you might take your driving theory test).
Cost: £65 for applicants who sit the test between 1st July and 31st August, £80 for applicants who sit the test between 1st September and 5th October; £100 for applicants sitting the test outside of the EU. Bursaries are available: for more information on these check the UCAT website.

Results: You will receive your UCAT score report on completing the test. Once you have submitted your UCAS application, you need to fill in your UCAS Personal Identification Number on your Pearson Vue UCAT account. They will then deliver your results to your chosen universities.

COMPOSITION OF THE UCAT

The UCAT consists of various sections which have been changed over the years. The whole test takes 2 hours and you are given your results immediately after the test.

Admissions Tests

In 2019 the test consisted of the following sections:

1 – Verbal Reasoning
This section assesses your ability to assimilate and consider written information. You will be given a series of 11 paragraphs to read, and asked to answer around 4 questions on each one. You are not expected to have any prior knowledge of the material, so even if you think you know the answer – forget it. The questions are based purely on the information in the passage and what inferences you can make from it. You may also be asked to select the statement that is the most logical conclusion from the passage, or specify what further information you would need in order to make a certain conclusion. There are 44 questions to be completed in 22 minutes.

2 – Decision-making
This section was introduced in 2017, to replace the previous section called Decision Analysis. It assesses your ability to make a logical and safe decision given complex information. The questions will be presented in reference to text, charts, tables, graphs or diagrams. Questions are standalone and utilise skills similar to the Verbal Reasoning section and the BMAT section 1. There are 29 questions in 32 minutes.

3 – Quantitative Reasoning
This section assesses your ability to assimilate and consider numerical information. You may be given sets of calculations to carry out from a table or graph, or asked to perform mental mathematics quickly. The information needed will all be there, but there will also be other irrelevant data. This means you have to figure out quickly what information you need, extract it, and then make your calculations. You are given a basic on-screen calculator to use and it is worth familiarising yourself with its format before doing the test. You have 25 minutes to complete 36 questions.

4 – Abstract Reasoning
This section assesses your ability to find relationships between sets of data and information. There are 4 types of question in this section, and all follow the same basic principles of pattern recognition and logic. The first type of question asks you to say whether the shape in question fits Set A or Set B better. The second type asks you to select the next shape in a series. The third type asks you to complete a set with a single shape.

Finally, the fourth type asks you to allocate 4 shapes to either Set A or Set B. There are 55 questions to complete in 14 minutes.

4 – Situational Judgement

This section assesses your capacity to understand real-life situations, appropriately prioritise various matters, and suggest a sensible course of action. This section is similar some of the clinical exams you will take later in your medical school career to help determine where you will have your first job. There are two sets of questions: the first asks you to determine the appropriateness of an action in response to a scenario, and the second asks you to assess the importance of an action in response to a scenario. Knowing the GMC's Good Medical Practice guide can help with this section, and it will also be useful when considering the short- and long-term solutions. The questions are about what you should do in a given scenario, not what you are more likely to do. There are 69 questions in 27 minutes.

HOW DO UNIVERSITIES USE THE UCAT?

Like the BMAT, this varies. Some will specify a cut-off mark, below which candidates will not receive an interview; others will use the UCAT score in conjunction with the rest of the application. Generally, the universities compare their applicants' scores and rank them accordingly. Contact individual universities or check the UCAT website for a detailed breakdown by university and course.

EXAMPLE QUESTIONS

Section 1

EuroDisney has reported more visitors but posted a net loss of €63m for the year ending September 30th. This was down from a small profit of €1.7 million in the same period in 2008.

While there were 15.45 million visitors in 2009, up from 15.3 million, customers are spending less than they have done in previous years, particularly with an increase in special offers. Guests, on average, spent €44.22, down 4.5% from last year, and the occupancy rate at the park's hotels slipped to 87.3% from 90.9%.

In the six months to 31st March 2010, the group's net earnings fell by 32% to €95.2 million ($121 million; £82 million) from sales that were down by 7%.

The group, which is 40% owned by the Walt Disney Company, said it had deferred payment of €25 million royalties and management fees and converted it to long-term subordinated debt, which will give it additional breathing space in the difficult economic environment.

The situation in the most recent year was "the most challenging economic environment in our history," said Philippe Gas, the EuroDisney Chief Executive. "We entered the downturn late – in April 2009 – and we will come out of it late. I don't expect a change before Spring."

Mr Gas added that the weak pound did not help, although, earlier this year, EuroDisney devised a scheme which allowed British holidaymakers to pay for their trip in pounds in advance.

Source: Various

1. EuroDisney has seen its net earnings fall to €63 million.
    - True
    - False
    - Can't tell

2. Special offers have attracted more visitors to Euro Disney in the past year.
    - True
    - False
    - Can't tell

Section 2

Questions 1-2 refer to the information and table below.

Mary owns a clothes shop in the West Midlands. After Christmas, she decides to run a sale on some of the items in the shop. The reductions are as follows:

Pre-sale	Post-sale
Anoraks £22.00	£17.60
Pyjamas £19.50	
Socks £3.00	£2.10
Hairbands £1.50	£0.90
T-shirts £8.00	£6.00

1. Mary chose to take 35% off the initial price of the pyjamas in the sale. What was their pre-sale price?
    A. £26.33
    B. £28.75
    C. £30.00
    D. £32.50
    E. £55.71

2. Which item's price was reduced by the largest percentage?
    A. Anoraks
    B. Pyjamas
    C. Socks
    D. Hairbands
    E. T-shirts

Section 3

For each question, decide whether the boxes below fit with Set A, Set B or neither. Answer 'A' for Set A, 'B' for Set B, or C for neither.

Questions 1-5

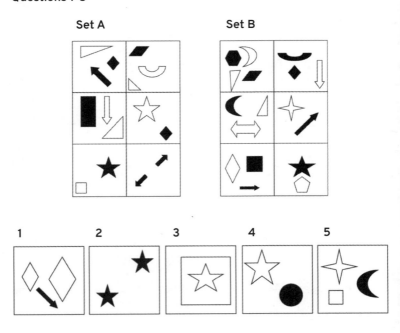

Section 4

Scenario:

A cipher expert has been found dead at his home. There were signs of a disturbance and his papers have been rummaged through, implying that the circumstances surrounding his death may be suspicious. You are the chief investigator of the police team looking into the demise of the cipher expert, and must start this process by wading through the wealth of papers in the flat. Unfortunately, it seems that this man took his work home with him: everything is in code. One list of codes seems to decipher a lot of papers – friends say that when the cipher expert was alive he referred to it as "standard code".

1 Dark	A Opposite
2 Food	B Later
3 Day	C More
4 Family	D Less
5 Job	E Single
6 Animal	F End
7 Sun	G Lower
8 Sleep	H Higher
9 Wash	I Own
10 Building	J Before
11 Body	K After
12 Liquid	L Without
13 Street	M Extreme
14 Car	
15 Clean	
16 Appointment	
17 Walk	

Choose which of the options is the best representation of the code found in the deceased man's diary?

1) 4,2,(K3)

1. Friends are coming for dinner later
2. Parents are having dinner after today
3. Parents are coming for dinner tomorrow
4. Parents are coming for dinner next week
5. I will eat my family tomorrow

Section 5

Mark the box that you agree with the most for each of the statements below:

	False	Somewhat False	Somewhat True	True
1. I am anxious before exams				
2. I feel guilty if I do not get to apologise to someone if I have done something wrong				
3. I find it hard to concentrate on something crucial if there are external distractions				
4. I consider myself to be more intelligent than my friends				
5. I do not judge individuals on their appearance				
6. I enjoy a routine				
7. I work best under stress				
8. I am good at multitasking				
9. I enjoy buying new things				
10. I take more pleasure in doing something I know how to do well than in doing something new not as proficiently				

Graduate Australian Medical School Admissions Test (GAMSAT)

The GAMSAT is a written examination specifically for applicants to Graduate Entry Medicine at certain universities. It consists of 3 sections taking 5½ hours in total, and is designed to test reasoning ability and critical thinking, reflective of the Problem-based Learning (PBL)-heavy courses at the schools that use it.

When: The GAMSAT takes place twice every year in the UK, in March and September. All candidates sit the test on the same day around the world. You may sit the test as many times as you like and use your best score, as long as it is achieved within the valid time period for your application.

Where: The test centres depend on the sitting, so check the GAMSAT website for the exact details. In the past, London, Liverpool, Dublin and Bristol (Europe) and Melbourne, Perth, Brisbane and Sydney (Australia) have been used. Singapore and Washington DC are offered on some cycles.

Cost: The amount is dependent on where you sit the test. For Europe and Australia, the fee is £255 if you register for the initial deadline, with an extra £60 cost if you register late. There is an additional fee when sitting the test in Singapore or Washington DC.

Results: You will be given an individual score for each section, and an overall GAMSAT score which is a weighted average of the three section scores. The overall GAMSAT score will be calculated using the following formula: Overall Score = (1 x Section I + 1 x Section II + 2 x Section III) ÷ 4. These results will be given online. Once you have provided your UCAS Personal Identification Number the results will be delivered to your chosen universities.

COMPOSITION OF THE GAMSAT

There are three sections in the test:

Section 1 – Reasoning in Humanities and Social Sciences
This section examines your skill in understanding and interpreting ideas in social/cultural contexts. There are usually written passages with some additional tables or visual information. There are 75 multiple-choice questions (MCQs) to complete in 100 minutes.

Section 2 – Written Communication
This section tests candidates' ability to develop and produce written ideas under time pressure. Task A asks for an essay that is analytical in style, and focused on socio-cultural issues. Task B asks candidates to write in a personal style on more familiar issues. There are 2 essays to write in 60 minutes.

Section 3 – Reasoning in Biological and Physical Sciences
This section uses questions from the sciences – roughly 40% biology, 40% chemistry, and 20% physics. The questions are set at approximately the level of 1st-year undergraduate biology/chemistry and A Level Physics. Questions will use passages, tables and other visual data. They will test problem-solving ability within scientific scenarios, asking for candidates to select reasonable hypotheses/conclusions, and draw appropriate connections. There are 110 MCQs in 170 minutes.

HOW IS THE GAMSAT SCORED AND USED?
Overall Score Calculation = (1 x Section I + 1 x Section II + 2 x Section III) / 4
This score remains valid for 2 years. Medical schools may use a cut-off mark in the GAMSAT as a requirement for entry.

EXAMPLE QUESTIONS AND REVISION
The examination board ACER supplies 4 booklets of sample questions, which will help applicants ascertain the level they need to be working at. The key to GAMSAT is to revise the relevant areas and practise the right style of essay writing. The GAMSAT is not easy, and has a large syllabus for the science sections, so efficient revision is essential.

7 MEDICAL SCHOOL INTERVIEWS

Medical School Interviews

To be a successful doctor, you need to be able to remain calm in stressful situations, adapt and work well in unknown circumstances, and be able to listen and communicate effectively. These are the skills being tested in most medical interviews.

Due to the high numbers of candidates applying for medical school, interviews are often the crucial decision-maker in whether you are successful in gaining a place. There is no 'secret formula' for excelling in an interview: the key is to be prepared to the best of your ability.

In this chapter we describe the basic structure and expectations of the different medical interviews; in the following chapter we tackle the details of the questions to might be asked and show you how to construct a compelling response.

WHAT ARE ADMISSIONS TUTORS LOOKING FOR IN AN INTERVIEW?

Tutors are looking for medical students who are committed and dedicated to becoming a doctor. This means the applicants need to be not only academically gifted, but also able to show the qualities required to become an excellent and gifted medical student (and future doctor).

The interviewers will expect you to be a little nervous, but it is important that you utilise any nerves and turn them into a successful performance.

HOW CAN I PREPARE FOR AN INTERVIEW?

To be successful, you have to be prepared for almost any question or situation, and be able to move quickly and intelligently in your thoughts and actions.

The best way to begin is to return to your Personal Statement and ensure that you have revised any books or research you have written about. Ideally, you should do extra reading to show you have researched each topic a little further – in case the interviewer asks about other books you have read.

Ensure that you have researched the university and understand the course, explaining why this course is ideal for you. Practise answering the typical questions you may be asked – for example: "Why have you chosen medicine?" However, do remember that it is important to sound natural and unrehearsed in the interview, so be able to adapt what you have practised.

Keep up-to-date with current affairs and GMC guidance. This is important to show your dedication to medicine, and that you are aware of the realities facing doctors at the moment.

Practise analysing articles so that you can quickly read a piece, extract the vital information and be able to present this in a professional manner. Also practise discussing ethical pieces, concentrating your discussion on the 'Four Principles of Medical Ethics'.

Have as many practise interviews as possible. The more interviews you can have with different people, the more confident and prepared you will feel for any question that could be asked. Practise interviews will also help you to deliver your answers in a concise and structured way. Remember not to be scared of saying 'I don't know' to a question, but be willing to try and work towards an answer with help from the interviewer. Finally, try to be refreshed for your interview: ensure you have a good night's sleep and arrive at the interview with plenty of time. Take deep breaths and remember: this is your time to shine. You have been good enough to get an interview, and if you have prepared well you have good reason to be confident that you will secure a place at medical school.

WHO WILL INTERVIEW ME?

You may be interviewed by a variety of people including academics, doctors, senior medical students and laypeople.

The interviewers could be your future lecturers or tutors, so they will be looking to see whether they feel they could teach you and whether you would suit the university's style of teaching.

WHAT WILL I BE EXPECTED TO KNOW?

Interviewers could ask you any question on any topic. However, they tend to ask questions and discuss topics related to the following categories:

- Critical thinking and problem-solving – including your ability to organise and prioritise.
- Integrity and resilience – how you cope with stressful situations.
- Communication skills including role-play.
- Practical stations to see how well you follow instructions or interpret data.
- Ethics and current affairs.
- Situational judgement – a question will be asked and you will have to ascertain whether a certain answer is (for example) always acceptable, sometimes acceptable or never acceptable; then explain why.
- Traditional questions – Why Medicine? Why this university? Discuss points on your Personal Statement, especially about your work experience. How have you shown your dedication to medicine so far?

Interviews are your chance to show the assessor the dedication and skills that would make you a fantastic doctor in the future.

WHAT ARE THE DIFFERENT STYLES OF INTERVIEWS USED?

Multiple Mini nterviews (MMI)

This is now the most common type of interview used by universities. The interview process consists of a series of short interviews ('stations') lasting on average between 7-9 mins each. After each station you will move on to the next, following a circuit until you have completed all stations. Each interview will be assessed by a different person who will then give a mark for that station. Typically, there is one interviewer per station, but be prepared: there may be more.
The benefit of the MMI format is that if one station doesn't go as well as you hoped, you have the opportunity to start afresh on the next station.

The drawback is that you have less control over the interview, as you only have a few minutes to excel and show your skills.
MMIs are representative of OSCEs (Objective Structured Clinical Examinations) – the style of exam you will take throughout medical school.

Traditional Interviews

Cambridge, Oxford and a small number of other universities still carry out the more traditional form of interview. This means staying in one room for 20-40 minutes, being interviewed by only one group of assessors (usually two, but occasionally a panel).

The benefit of a traditional interview is that it allows more time to build rapport with the interviewers and gain confidence. In addition, you have more time to express your thoughts and ideas, as there is usually no set time limit. The drawback is that if you feel it is going badly, then unfortunately you do not get a fresh start after a few minutes like in the MMIs.

The majority of a Cambridge/Oxford interview will be scientifically based, so it is important to ensure that your knowledge of your A Level subjects (or equivalent) is exceptional.

Example questions for both styles of interview

1. **Organising/Prioritising**
   The ward you are working on is short-staffed and you are asked to work extra hours during the week to cover this. You also have an important football match at the weekend, for which the coach requires you to have extra training in the week. You also have plans to go to the cinema, and a party with friends. How would you deal with this situation?

2. **Communication skills**
   You are a junior doctor working on a surgery firm. Mr Smith is due for an operation on his hernia at 11am. He has been nil by mouth since midnight. However, due to a bed shortage his operation has been cancelled. You have been given the task of explaining this to Mr Smith. (No specialist knowledge of surgery or hernias is required for this question.)

3. **Interpreting data**
   A graph is presented to you showing levels of cancer in developing and developed countries. You may be asked to explain the differences in the data.

4. **Ethics**
   Mr Brown is very ill in hospital; the tests have revealed he has

advanced bowel cancer. His family have asked you not to tell him the results of the tests, as they feel if he knew he would fail to cope and it would cause him extreme distress. What would you do? What if Mr Brown asked you about his diagnosis?

5. Current affairs

How should we deal with medical tourism? How do you feel about the new junior doctor contract? What are your thoughts on NIPT?

The above is a brief survey of the sorts of problems posed in the medical interviews: in the next chapter we look at some of these in more detail.

8 APPROACHING INTERVIEW QUESTIONS

Approaching Interview Questions

This chapter should help you think through some of the questions you might face in an interview, and decide how to structure an answer to them. There are few absolutely right or wrong answers – but certain approaches or answers will win you more points than others. Each year the interviewers come up with a host of new questions and topics to push and challenge applicants, and here we list some interview questions based on feedback from recent students. Medical questions will require you to use existing knowledge and apply it in a new situation, as well as demonstrating a strong foundation of knowledge from school learning and further reading as outlined in your Personal Statement.

Different medical schools hold different types of interview, and here we will go through some example questions to give you an overview of what might come up in each one. Oxford and Cambridge still hold old-fashioned science-focused interviews, as well as more individual-centric interviews like the other medical schools. The Multiple Mini Interview (MMI) is now very common and used across the country as a way to efficiently assess candidates in a range of unseen situations. There are some constants across the country – not least the staple questions of "Why Medicine?" and "What do you know and like about this medical school?"

While we may focus on certain questions here, there are no guarantees as to what will be asked. The purpose of considering the questions is rather to explore the logical and creative thinking skills required to succeed at interview. The approaches outlined below are by no means perfect 'model answers': they outline an approach to questions that you can adapt to different situations.

We have split up the styles of question to facilitate your use of this chapter, but there is often some overlap between them. For example, there is often little distinction between 'ethical' and 'science' questions – you may be asked questions that contain elements of both.

THE OBVIOUS QUESTIONS

There are some questions that every candidate should prepare for, and for which a good candidate will have a well-structured and innovative response.

- "Why Medicine?"

Many interviews begin with a question along these lines as a way to set the candidate at ease, and thereby help them through the rest of the interview. It is a challenging question because for many students, there is no one single reason that they want to study medicine – perhaps it is an idea they have had for so long that it is impossible to pinpoint one exact event that led to your application. Some candidates, by contrast, may have a specific reason or experience. For example: perhaps a loved one developed a condition, and they were amazed by the work of the doctors, wanting to become one ever since.

The interviewers will hear countless answers to this question, so being able to stand out here is hard. The best answers come from students who have thought long and hard about why they have made this decision, and who can distil that into a punchy, minute-long answer. Good answers come from those who have something interesting to say, and who are genuinely passionate about studying medicine. The danger here can be to go on for too long or talk a bit aimlessly: hence the need for preparation and concision.

- "What do you know/like about the course here?"

Every university wants students who want to be there. It is your job to convince the interviewers that you are going to make good use of the educational opportunities while also contributing to and engaging with other things on offer at the university.

It reflects poorly on a candidate if they cannot name any reasons that they chose this specific university for Medicine, or if they do not know the general outline of what and how they might be studying for the next five or six years. These are very simple matters to look up, and there are many opportunities to show your knowledge – for instance, you could talk about the nature of the course (integrated or preclinical/clinical), the campus location, a specific module that you think sounds particularly interesting, or the reputation and prestige that the university and course hold.

- "Tell us about something you've read recently."

Every prospective student applying for Medicine should be up-to-date with the latest news, ranging from the NHS to cutting-edge medical research. You probably wrote something about current medical affairs in your Personal Statement; the ability to talk about these topics indicates that you have a high level of initiative and are heavily involved in your own learning.

There are many sources of information, largely splitting into books, popular articles and academic articles. Books should be mentioned in your Personal Statement and will have informed you on various aspects of medicine over the last few years. Popular articles are just what you read on the BBC homepage every day and in your New Scientist subscription. Academic articles are for those with a keen interest in science and who have a specific area of expertise, such as cancer, with which they try to stay up-to-date. All three can form good answers to a question about your reading.

When answering a question like this, keep in mind why the interviewer is asking it – they want to find other things out about you. Does this student care about medicine? Can they condense an article into a simple explanation? Do they understand (or have they tried hard to understand) what the author was really trying to say?

When reading books or articles, it is therefore a good idea to make notes as you go along to help jog your memory and aid understanding. It can also be good practise to write a short summary of it at the end, as a way to prepare for questions like this.

- "What do you think is the most important breakthrough in medical history?"

This branch of questions assesses whether you have a grasp of the place that medicine holds in human history, and what your priorities are in studying medicine. There are many answers to a question like this, and indeed several books have been written on the subject. Cases can be made for all of the following, which you can research at home:

- Penicillin
- Anaesthetics
- Soap
- X-rays
- VF
- Banning smoking in certain places
- Sewerage systems
- Vaccination – e.g. MMR or smallpox
- Antiseptics
- Insulin
- Birth control

For this question, it is interesting to consider the various options and how they might relate to each other. For example, penicillin was groundbreaking because it meant that many previously fatal conditions could now be completely cured. However, you could contrast this to soap, which essentially allowed people to have better hygiene and thus spread disease less in the first place. Soap was also discovered long before penicillin, and so could be said to have a greater contribution to mankind's health.

- "Can you explain a time that you demonstrated good teamwork/ leadership skills?"

Teamwork and leadership are buzzwords in the NHS, and with good cause. The ability to be a team player is essential in any doctor's practice, and at various points throughout your career you will have to step up and take charge. Many students highlight these qualities in their Personal Statement, using examples from their lives as part of the sports team or orchestra. It's also possible to use other examples to illustrate your point, such as challenges in your home life or volunteering placements.

The essential point is that you need to demonstrate a willingness to sacrifice glory or personal success in order that the team win together. Some students struggle with this, but medical teams must work together to save the life of patients – there is no personal winner if you don't win together.

- "Tell me about _____ on your Personal Statement."

Every single thing you have written on your Personal Statement is fair game for an interviewer to ask you about. Even if you intended to mention some particular condition as a throwaway comment, you may be incredibly lucky (or unlucky!) to have a national expert on that condition across from you at the table.

If you say that you have read something, make sure you have read it and are at least able to talk about it in some detail. You could practise explaining the main argument of the author, or the exact chapters or ideas that particularly struck you when you were reading it. Did it change your opinion about something? Did it confirm pre-existing thoughts?

When you write about a work experience placement, make sure you have something interesting to say about it. Can you talk about an interaction you observed and learnt something from? Can you explain a condition that you hadn't heard of before the junior doctor told you about it on a lunch break?

This way of thinking about your experiences applies to any idea or event that you discuss in your statement. Before the interview, make sure you know what you wrote inside out, and hopefully these questions will be a gift.

ETHICAL QUESTIONS

Ethical questions are a mainstay at every medical school, and ask you to use your analytical abilities and your knowledge of medical ethics to suggest appropriate courses of action. These questions are not necessarily about being 'right' or 'wrong': medical situations that are the subject of ethical dilemmas may have arguments on both sides. Here, interviewers are looking for the capacity to take in information, weigh it up, and suggest a solution.

Worked Example

Q) If there was only one bird flu vaccine left, who should get it: you or me?

A) You might first start by explaining what you understand by the question. "Bird flu is a potentially fatal strain of flu, related to an avian influenza virus, for which we have developed a vaccine. Receiving the vaccine would hopefully prevent contraction of the the illness, which might start with fever and muscle pain but then potentially progress to something more serious."

At this point you could start analysing which of the student and interviewer should receive it. There are many factors to consider here – for example:
- Are either of you immunocompromised? This would be affected by:
  – Age
  – Pregnancy
  – Immunosuppressive drugs
  – Chemotherapy
  – HIV infection
- Have either of you had bird flu before and thus developed immunity?
- Whose illness or death would be cause more problems? Do either of you have any dependents who might also suffer if you were sick?
- Do either of you suffer from anything else that will already shorten your life expectancy?

Having explored some of these factors, you could reach a conclusion. At this stage, there are two options for you.

First, if you feel that you do not have enough information to make an absolute decision as to who should receive the vaccine, it is OK to say that. You could conclude that without further information about the interviewer's health and general circumstances, you could not make an informed decision in this scenario and be able to stand by it 100 per cent.

However, if you are someone who would rather not sit on the fence, you could equally conclude with: "Assuming that we are both of the same health and circumstances, I may give it to myself, because I am younger than you and would therefore derive more benefit from the vaccine."

Examples for you to try yourself

Q) A patient with multiple sclerosis has come to you asking for help in ending his life due to the severe disability and pain he now suffers from. What do you do?

Q) Some trusts want to refuse surgery to obese patients. Should this be allowed?

Q) There are three people on the kidney transplant register who are all well matched to a kidney that has recently become available. Patient A is a 75-year-old man, Patient B is a 30-year-old woman, and Patient C is a 10-year-old boy. You may ask me as many questions as you like, but in 2 minutes I would like you to tell me who should receive the kidney.

Q) The world is becoming quickly overpopulated, and yet the NHS funds IVF in some areas. Is this contributing to the problem? Should doctors be encouraging the public to adopt rather than have fertility treatment?

Q) A 14-year-old girl is sleeping with her 15-year-old boyfriend, and has come to you, a GP, asking for a prescription for the oral contraceptive. What do you do?

Q) Should a doctor ever tell a patient that they will be completely cured?

SCIENCE QUESTIONS

These questions are the foundation of the interview at Oxford and Cambridge, and still form a component of interviews elsewhere. Here you will be assessed on your pre-existing scientific knowledge and, more specifically, how you can apply and communicate that. The scope is very broad here, covering much of A Level Biology and Chemistry, and also including whatever diseases or scientific topics may have been mentioned on your Personal Statement.

Worked Example

Q) What makes HIV/AIDS an interesting disease from the perspective of a doctor?

A) A good answer to this question would be one that first addresses the biology of the disease. You could start by mentioning the fact that HIV/ AIDS affects the immune system and renders the patient more vulnerable to other opportunistic infections. This would be an opportunity for you to display your knowledge of the immune system, and the fact that HIV infects CD4 cells specifically. You could also mention that it is difficult to treat because of the virus' ability to rapidly develop resistance to drugs. Don't be afraid to ask about the biological aspect of HIV/AIDS if you don't know the science of the disease: the interviewers will appreciate your interest and the fact that you are making an effort.

To address the question from another angle, you could discuss where HIV/AIDS is a significant problem geographically – remember to give your definition of "significant" in your answer! Sub-Saharan Africa currently has a high incidence of HIV/AIDS, as do parts of Asia. In these countries, the disease is often transmitted via sexual networks that include prostitutes and drug users. The social stigma of infection can act as a barrier both to treatment, and to the prevention of onwards transmission. Transmission of HIV has been linked to poverty in the countries with high prevalence rates. As an example, women driven to prostitution may be unable to refuse sex because it may be their main source of income. If condoms are unavailable or considered undesirable for whatever reason, these women may be at great risk.

HIV/AIDS creates problems within societies because it leaves orphans in its wake when parents die of the disease. Further, the disease may be transmitted to babies during pregnancy, creating HIV-positive children at birth. This means that governments need to find ways of caring for orphaned HIV-positive children, who require general everyday care and treatment for the disease.

There are interesting instances of misinformation about transmission of HIV/AIDS. For example, some men believe that their disease can be cured by sexual intercourse with virgins, an act which may infect the women that they have sex with. Also, some people avoid condoms because they are associated with the infection itself. HIV/AIDS is stigmatised in many communities, so infection is often traumatic for both the patient and their family.

As you can see from the first paragraph here, there is plenty to say about HIV even from a purely biological perspective. However, you can extend this further by demonstrating your understanding that HIV/AIDS has much wider social, cultural and economic implications, all of which play an important role in the transmission, treatment and prevention of the disease. This is still of importance to a doctor: someone who is ultimately concerned for the health and wellbeing of all in a society.

Examples for you to try yourself

Q) What is the purpose of DNA, and how does it relate to RNA?

Q) How would you design a brain? Is the skull appropriate to its function?

Q) How does insulin work?

Q) What makes bacteria as successful as they are?

Q) What is a mitochondrion? Why do you only inherit mitochondrion genes from your mother?

Q) Why may a drug not have the same effect on a human as on a cat?

Q) How are fish adapted to their environment? Could a human develop those adaptations?

CRITICAL THINKING QUESTIONS
Many interviews will ask you to quickly assimilate new information and analyse it critically and sensibly. This can be in a scientific context, or in looking at more general social and cultural trends.

The interviewers are looking for an ability to think on your feet and apply your existing knowledge to a problem. It is easy to miss something obvious in these questions, so just think out loud and show your line of reasoning. If you have an initial answer straightaway, it may be wise to bite your tongue and just think through the problem systematically.

When given graphical information, it is important to remember that correlation does not always imply causation in either direction. Two factors can be associated without any significant connection between them, either because some further factor (or factors) explains the association, or even just due to simple coincidence (something that

malarial mosquitos, and a surge in infection requiring drastic action.
2. A virus that recurs biennially could be due to mutations that cause cyclical outbreaks, such as with the flu. The influenza virus mutates every year and every year humans produce a new vaccine; only sometimes is it effective.
3. Graph 3 could be the same factor that occurs three times in 30 years, such as three particularly harsh winters or wet summers; or it could be three totally separate factors causing three independent recurrences.

Examples for you to try yourself
Q) In the UK, 60% of medical students are currently female. Do you think we should have equal quotas for medical school places for men and women? What do you think will be the consequences of having more female doctors than male doctors?

Q) More and more people are becoming overweight and obese. What is causing this and what can we do about it?

Q) If you were on a desert island and could take three medical items with you, in addition to food, shelter and water, what would you choose?

Q) The graph below shows average heights for world regions from 1810 to 1980. What trends do you see, and can you comment on the relative contribution of environment and genetics using this graph?

NHS-RELATED QUESTIONS
Medical schools are training the next generation of doctors, and as such they must ensure that any applicants have a keen and vested interest in the health service of this country. The NHS is constantly undergoing changes that will be directly affecting incoming students by the time they qualify. An appreciation of the topical problems faced by doctors in the NHS is key, and failure to answer a question on these areas well could severely hinder a candidate.

A good answer on this topic may also reflect your engagement with doctors of various levels during your work experience, thus gaining an 'onthe-ground' understanding.

scientific experiments account for by repeatability of results).

Worked Example

Q) Imagine a frequency graph of three different viruses over a 30-year period. One gradually increases and decreases; one peaks every other year; and one peaks three times within a 30-year period. Why?

A)   With a question like this, the information is clearly visually interpretable, but there is no graph given to you – so draw the graph! Don't be afraid to check what you have drawn with the interviewer, and ask for clarification if you are struggling.

1.
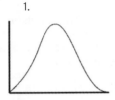

2.

3.
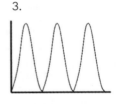

You could next outline the factors that affect frequency of viral infection in a population – for example:

- Climate – changes in temperature, humidity, seasons.
- Mutation of the virus – this could improve transmission or increase drug resistance
- Other viruses – competition or symbiosis (e.g. infection with the influenza virus weakens the immune system and increases the chance of other infections)
- Discovery of a vaccine
- Control methods such as vector eradication

With this list, you could then look at each graph and consider what factor might explain it. An example is always a good idea, and the interviewer may help you along if you are going in the wrong direction.

1.   A vaccine could explain graph 1 with a sudden decrease in numbers – this was seen in smallpox, a disease that is now eradicated. Another explanation of graph 1 could be environmental change – for example, a warming of the UK climate leading to migration of

Worked Example

Q) If you were the new Secretary of State for Health, how would you want to improve the NHS?

A) This is a highly personal question, and one that could be taken in many directions. Options include:

- Addressing long waiting times for surgeries and scans
- Tackling the prevalence of super-bugs such as MRSA and C. difficile
- Tackling low retention rates of doctors post-graduation – many leave to work in commercial services or emigrate to work as a doctor abroad
- Addressing lack of funding for services in the community such as GUM clinics
- Reducing the incidence of events such as bed sores and falls in hospital – avoidable issues that severely hinder recovery
- Creating more bed space within hospitals by funding care homes for the many elderly patients that cannot be discharged
- Promoting public health issues such as the rise of obesity and diabetes, and making policy changes to encourage children to be more active
- Smoking
- Tackling issues with bureaucracy and computer systems
- The question does not specify how many things you can improve, and so a good candidate will explore some of the options above, developing a few of them further.

For example, you might begin by talking about the problems of treating conditions that have arisen through lifestyle – such as the high incidence of diabetes and how this has a knock-on effect on many other conditions. You could talk about how it is ultimately cheaper to prevent someone from getting a disease than it is to treat them for it. This is almost universally true: for example, teaching better hand hygiene nationally can reduce the transmission of colds and flu; educating about the dangers of smoking can prevent people from developing COPD and lung cancer; schemes that provide free condoms help prevent the transmission of STIs such as chlamydia and syphilis. As Secretary of State for Health, it would be your prerogative to make real changes in these realms: for example, by increasing the number of alcohol gel dispensers in public places around the country, or improving training for hospital staff who sterilise and clean equipment.

Examples for you to try yourself

Q) Tell me what you know about the dispute over the Junior Doctors' Contract in 2016.

Q) How is an MRI scan for a cancer patient funded?

Q) What is the role of a GP, and how does it differ from that of a hospital consultant?

Q) What is similar about being a doctor 50 years ago and being one today? What is different?

Q) Should doctors play a role in the regulation of contact sports such as American Football or boxing?

Q) Does holistic medicine fall under the auspices of the NHS?

Q) Why are you applying to be a doctor and not another health professional such as a nurse?

QUESTIONS ABOUT YOU

Interviewers will want to know more about how YOU have come to apply for Medicine at their university, and why YOU would make a good doctor. They will use a range of questions to learn more about you, which we can roughly divide into (a) work experience and volunteering; (b) communication skills; (c) the attributes of a doctor; and (d) the Personal Statement. You will notice that there is a lot of overlap between these questions and the questions mentioned in the previous sections.

WORK EXPERIENCE & VOLUNTEERING

Medical interviews differ from other subjects because they are often carried out by actual doctors, rather than academics – one of the virtues of a vocational course. In an interview, you are being assessed both for your suitability to the Medicine course and for your suitability to a medical career. You can show both when answering all these styles of questions, but talking about your work experience is a good way to demonstrate it strongly.

When it comes to questions, interviewers tend to leave them quite open, saying something like: "Tell me about your work experience." Many students fall into the trap of listing all the different hospitals and surgeries they have visited, thinking that this sounds impressive. What is more interesting to interviewers, however, is not the quantity of experience you have, but the quality. Tutors want to hear about an experience where you learned what it means to be a doctor, and about the relationship that doctors build with their patients.

Another possibility is that a question doesn't sound at all related to work experience, but is in fact an excellent place to mention it.

Good applicants might therefore approach this type of question by mentioning their observation of the importance of good communication – seeing a doctor smiling or softening their body language as they greeted the patient, all helping to make the patient feel more relaxed. Initially, doctors often won't know what they're looking for and must rely on the openness of the patient to tell them their complaint. You may have seen how a doctor will use simple layman's terms with a patient, refraining from medical jargon and thereby ensuring the patient understands what is going on at every step of their treatment. It may be that during your work experience you observed how important the wider team is to the doctor's role: for example, how much the nurses and radiographers help in the overall process. The options are endless and, of course, it all depends on your actual experience.

You might also have seen some of the negative aspects of being a doctor, including the amount of paperwork involved, the strain of having to deliver bad news to a patient, or the long hours. You may have seen how important it is for a doctor to be able to detach themselves emotionally from the case. All of these are valuable observations and show that you were engaged with your work experience.

Much of this advice also applies to volunteering, and will again depend on the placement you had and your particular engagement with it. It is likely that you were able to get more involved in your volunteering placement than you could at your medical work experience, so you should be able to draw on more first-hand material: for example, what you learnt about how you can personally build a relationship with someone who struggles to communicate.

In general, think hard about what you learned and how it changed, strengthened or weakened certain opinions on the doctor's role that you may have previously held.

Examples for you to try yourself
Q) Tell me about a doctor that either impressed or shocked you.

Q) What skills did you develop on your placement that you think will help you in the daily life of a doctor?

Q) Having seen the workload and dedication of nurses, do you think it's fair that they get paid less than doctors?

Q) How do you think doctors develop the resilience to see people suffering every day?

Q) If your younger sibling were to apply to study medicine, which of your work experience placements would you recommend and why?

Q) Have any of the patients or service users you met while volunteering or on work experience stayed with you?

Q) Do you think work experience students should be allowed more clinical access and freedom on their placements?

COMMUNICATION
Communication is the art of much more than merely speaking. It encompasses a whole range of skills that all boil down to how well you can relate and convey information to another human. Good communication is essential to the working life of a doctor and it is something that all medical students must demonstrate. Doctors have to talk all day, every day with both patients and colleagues, and as such there is a huge premium on your ability to effectively communicate.

Much of this is assessed by your general performance at interview and at the questions seen above. Do not underestimate the importance of the ability to string together an intelligent, coherent sentence while maintaining good eye contact and smiling. At some universities, they will assess your ability to communicate in a scenario with an actor. The following should give you some points to consider when interacting with others in an interview scenario.

1. Communication skills are often innate – some people are better talkers than others – but that doesn't mean they can't be developed. Confidence plays a large role, and while it's understandable that you might be nervous at an interview, it's important that you try to minimise the effect your nerves can have. The best way to do this is with practise interviews: these help you see how you deal with the pressure and whether this impacts on your ability to communicate.

2. Knowing what communications skills the interviewers are concentrating on will also help you in the interview. For example: doctors are expected to give advice and manage a patient's treatment, but the patient has the right to choose, and to be well informed about their options. As a doctor, it will be your job to educate them about this, and help them to come to a decision that they are happy with. As a medical student, however, you may not be able to give comprehensive medical advice – you aren't expected to know the details of a treatment for diabetes, for example – but you are still well placed to listen to and support someone who is struggling with their recent diagnosis. This distinction is important and is central in what medical schools may be looking for: they care more about how you try to relate to a role-play actor/patient than about how much you actually know.

3. There is a balance to be found in the language you actually use. You should sound like you know what you are doing – avoid colloquialisms and slang. If there is a technical word that is appropriate, then you should use it. However, if the task is focused on communicating to a layperson or patient, avoid medical jargon and speak in clear and simple terms – this is ultimately what you will have to do as a doctor.

A communication checklist

Here are some key aspects of communication to remain aware of:

1. Structure your answers
   a. Make sure they're clearly laid out and that one point follows from the next.
   b. Answer the actual question.

    c. Avoid waffling – medical schools want to see that you can be succinct and clear, not using 5 minutes to say something you could convey in 30 seconds.

2. Body Language
   a. Avoid fidgeting.
   b. Maintain eye contact when appropriate.
   c. Dress like a doctor would – smart but comfortable.
   d. Non-verbal cues – such as nodding and smiling when someone says something.
   e. Sounds like "mmm" or "uhuh" indicate you're engaged in the conversation

3. Listening
   a. Listening is as important as speaking.
   b. Being an "active listener" is a skill that can be learnt and is something you should research further.

4. Empathy
   a. This is perhaps the most important communication skill.
   b. Indicating that you are trying to understand a patient's situation is one of the most powerful things a doctor can do.
   c. It is important to acknowledge that you can never know what another person is actually feeling – but you can still try to put yourself in their shoes.

Questions for you to try yourself

Q) Can good communication be learnt?

Q) Role Play Scenario: You are a delivery-person for Meat the Greek, a Greek fast-food restaurant. Meat the Greek has a 1-hour guarantee according to which a client doesn't have to pay for their food if it arrives more than one hour after they placed the order. On a delivery one night, you see an elderly man fall down in the street and cry out in pain. You know that if you don't make this delivery, you will lose your job (which you need to fund your studies).

- First: please explain to the examiner what you think you should do.

- Second: please explain this course of action to your boss, and deal with his questions.

Q) If you were to invite three people to dinner, who would they be and why?

Q) Role Play Scenario: A friend has confided in you that they have been feeling depressed recently, and they don't know what to do. Talk to them about how they're coping.

Q) What's more important: body language, or how articulate you are when speaking?

Q) A patient who has recently been given a liver transplant is taken out for dinner by a friend, who then offers to buy a bottle of wine to celebrate. How do you think the liver transplant recipient might feel about this?

Q) You are outside South Kensington Tube station in London and someone collapses in front of you. Someone goes to help him and calls you over. They ask you to call 999. Please talk to the operator, explain the situation and follow their instructions.

MULTIPLE MINI INTERVIEWS

The Multiple Mini Interview (MMI) is a relatively new format for interviews at medical school. It aims to emulate the clinical OSCE exams that students sit in the later years of university, and involves rotating around different stations. At each station you will be set a task to complete in the given time, and at the end of that time you will move to the next station. You repeat this process until all the candidates in the room have done all the stations. This general format varies in several ways: for example, how long each station lasts for; how many stations there are in total; and – obviously – what each station is asking you to do. MMIs contain a range of all the types of question discussed above, and it can be hard to predict what will show up – hence why great preparation is needed.

The physical format of an MMI is simple. The university will set up an area with around 6-12 stations, either behind screens or in separate adjoining rooms. Each of these stations is manned by an examiner and potentially an actor playing a role. Candidates will be told which station they are starting at. When the assessment begins, they will be given time to read the brief outside the station. When the buzzer goes, they will enter and begin, until the next buzzer indicates that the time is over. They are then given time to move to the next station or room, and again given some time to read the brief there.

Below are two example circuits for you to gain an appreciation of how these work. Many situations will develop as you go into them, particularly those with actors. This means that some briefs will seem very straightforward to begin with, and end up being quite complex as more information is given to you and the situation develops.

HOW TO USE THE CIRCUITS BELOW
For each station you will get 1 minute of reading time for the brief below, and then 6 minutes in the station. We recommend that you pair up with a friend, time yourself and go through these stations one by one, taking turns to be the actor, candidate and examiner.

MMI Circuit 1

Station 1
Without moving your hands from the table, please explain to the examiner how to sew a button onto a shirt.

Station 2
How would you set up a blood bank in a developing country? What problems might you face?

Station 3
Please talk to the patient in the room about her problems with alcohol.

Station 4
Tell the examiner about an event in your life where you feel you were really able to help someone.

Station 5
Please wash your hands and explain what you are doing at each stage. The examiner may guide you.

Station 6
You are in your first month of working at a butcher's as an assistant.

A customer comes in to collect the order she placed last week. She ordered a very specific cut of meat with you and explained that it is for a very complicated dish that she is cooking to impress her boss and her husband when they come for dinner. While you did place the order, you forgot to confirm its delivery date and you have just realised it will be arriving next week. This lady ordered it for today, as the dinner party is tonight. Please explain what has happened and sort out the situation.

Station 7
Please put on the blindfold when you enter and then describe the object the examiner hands to you. Please suggest what you think it is, and what it might be used for.

Station 8
You are given details of 10 schoolchildren that have been stranded on a desert island. You have the ability to save 5 of them from the island with a helicopter. Who do you save?

MMI Circuit 2

Station 1
Your younger brother has just kicked a football into your neighbour's garden while he was playing. Your neighbour is a grumpy 80-year-old man, and your brother asks you to go over and plead for his football back. Please talk to your neighbour to get your brother's ball back.

Station 2
What do you think is the biggest burden on the NHS today?

Station 3
Tell me about red blood cells and their adaptations to their function.

Station 4
A patient has come to you on crutches and during the consultation asks you for a disability permit for their car. You agree and sign off on it. When you leave work that evening, you see the same patient walking about easily, and without crutches. What do you do?

Station 5
Here is an article for you to read about the rates of smoking in the UK

and the effect smoking has on the lungs. Please explain this article to the patient inside who has been smoking for the last 40 years.

Station 6
A good friend from school has rung you in her second term of university and told you that she thinks she has contracted chlamydia. She has looked up all the symptoms and is convinced that her boyfriend of 4 years, who you also know from school, is cheating on her. Please pick up the phone inside and talk to her about this.

Station 7
Discuss a time that you felt overwhelmed by what was happening in your life and the strategies you used to cope with it.

Station 8
What is this and how does it work?

By virtue of the format, MMIs are not meant to be easy to prepare for. The best way to become better at interviews is to practise, and for the MMI this is especially true. While the range of questions that could come up is broad, the examiners are essentially trying to see what kind of person you are and whether you have the innate skills to be a good doctor. A central document to look at is Tomorrow's Doctors, published by the GMC, which can almost be thought of as a syllabus used by medical schools when setting interview questions. It outlines the expectations and requirements placed on doctors, and thus what students who are applying to medical school should be demonstrating.

MORE INTERVIEW QUESTIONS
- How does the replication of leading and lagging strands differ in DNA replication?
- What do you know about stem cells?
- Mutations in the mitochondrial DNA causes the male tissues of the plant to die. In the 2nd generation of this how would the frequency of the mutation change in the population?
- Talk to me about mitochondria.
- Tell me something that's interested you recently.
- Tell us about a hobby.
- How do anaesthetics work?
- Design an experiment to test the efficacy of a certain drug.

- Talk about a patient from work experience that you learnt something from.
- Describe 3 qualities of a doctor and give examples.
- Describe a practical you attempted that didn't work.
- Why do koalas have fur if they live in Australia?
- If you were a politician, what policies would you introduce to reduce the impact of air pollution, and what benefits would they have on the population?
- Why is a large portion of DNA not involved in coding for proteins?
- Why Medicine?
- Tell me about your work experience?
- What causes cancer?
- In what state does a cell spend most time in during mitosis?
- Tell me about tumour-suppressor/proto-oncogenes.
- What happens when there is a mutation in these genes?
- How do antibiotics work?
- How do antibiotics differentiate between virus and bacterial cells?
- What is the name of the nerve that decreases our heart rate?
- What recent scientific journal have you read?
- What is a gene, what does it do?
- What are codons and anticodons? Where are they found?
- What is an antigen and what are the body's defences against it?
- How do antibodies work and how are they so specific to each antigen?
- What is the difference between Dementia and Alzheimer's?
- What is HIV? How does it spread?
- How does HIV replicate?
- How does HIV treatment work?
- What is an angioplasty?
- Why do we have only one heart?
- Why is the liver on the right side of the body?
- Why is cancer becoming more prevalent? Do not mention ageing.
- As a scientist how would you use stem cells?
- How would your friends describe you? What are some of your weaknesses?
- Adapt a bacteria living at 37 degrees to live at 120 degrees.
- Why do amino acids exist as positive on the -NH2 side and negative on -COOH side?
- Why is cannibalism seen as something negative in our society?
- Mathematically, how does a cat see?

- What is your most memorable work experience case?
- What are the most important chemicals for life?
- What are the advantages to keyhole surgery?
- Why are arteries elastic?
- Can everyone give consent?
- How is memory stored?
- Discuss the mechanisms underlying diabetes.
- How would you decide who to give a liver to?
- Who do you think made the biggest contribution to modern Medicine?
- How would you design a brain?
- How have Doctor's lives changed in the last thirty years?
- What is a CAT scan?
- Should we charge smokers for their healthcare?
- What are ulcers?
- What do you know about Parkinson's disease? What about the treatment?
- How does researching yeast help medical science?
- Why is MRSA known as a superbug?
- What do you think of assisted suicide?
- Why do we have two eyes?
- 'Define perception.' Is perception the same as consciousness?
- What is the Kreb's cycle?
- Explain a difficult decision you've had to make in your life so far.
- Why does foetus lose mass directly after birth?
- What hormones are involved in the absorption of calcium into the bones?
- Tell me about appendicitis.
- What is cystic fibrosis?
- Talk about benzene chemistry.
- What is the GMC?
- Define a genome.
- What would life be like without enzymes?
- Why does the spine get thinner as it goes up?
- Discuss 'free energy.'
- Describe the humeral immune response.
- How does a foetus receive oxygen?
- How important is honesty in a doctor's work?
- What is a prion? How can we use prions?
- What is the function of the refractory period?

- How does TB spread?
- Why can't you tickle yourself?
- How has austerity affected the NHS?
- Why do older people fracture their bones more often?
- How would I measure the volume of this room?
- What is the function of alveoli and what are the possible problems?
- In terms of global health, how has war affected Medicine?
- Explain transport in the kidney.
- What stops action potentials being slow?
- What surrounds the brain?

9 GUIDANCE FOR INTERNATIONAL APPLICANTS

Guidance for International Applicants

In this final chapter we offer some guidance on navigating the application process as an overseas applicant.

You are classed as an international or overseas applicant if you are domiciled outside of the UK or EU. It does not matter where you hold a passport, as your status depends solely on your country of permanent residence. If you are unsure about whether you are an international or home applicant, the Admissions Office at each university to which you apply can clarify your status.

Here, we discuss the admission process for an international applicant, including information on language requirements, accepted qualifications, and visas.

ENGLISH LANGUAGE REQUIREMENTS

As Medicine courses are taught in English, all applicants must have a good verbal and written grasp of the language. If English is not your first language, but you have been in full-time education in the English language for the past two years, you may not need to sit a test, depending on your university choices. Otherwise, you may be asked to complete a formal qualification such as the IELTS or TOEFL. A list of acceptable Englishlanguage qualifications can be found on each university's website.

COUNTRY-SPECIFIC QUALIFICATIONS

Many international qualifications are recognised by UK universities, but not all are accepted by every university. It is important to visit the university websites to ensure that your qualification type makes you eligible to make an application. The main thing to bear in mind is that you will need to be studying science to a high level: particularly Biology and Chemistry, but also Mathematics. You can get a statement about how your qualifications compare to UK qualifications from the UK National Recognition Information Centre.

UCAS (UNIVERSITIES AND COLLEGES ADMISSIONS SERVICE)

Every student applying to a UK medical school must submit their application through UCAS. From mid-September, you can apply to UK universities online. You can use the UCAS service from anywhere in the world: find out more information at www.ucas.com.

Your application does not have to be completed in one session; you can return to it later and change or add information before you submit it. However, you will need to mark every section of the form as complete before you can send your application to UCAS. The application deadline for Medicine, Veterinary Medicine, and most Dentistry courses is 15th October of the year before you aim to begin studying.

ACADEMIC REFERENCES

As part of your application, you will need a reference highlighting your academic and personal suitability for the Medicine course. This will usually be written by a teacher from your current school who knows you well and can provide an accurate account of your abilities. A full written reference is required (name and address are not sufficient), and must be written in English. If you are applying through a school, college or other organisation, you will not have access to your reference: it will be completed on your behalf by your referee and sent directly through UCAS to your chosen universities.

If you are applying as an individual, you need to ensure that the reference section is completed in good time, as you will not be able to send your application through UCAS without it. If you are applying independently but would like your reference to be written by a registered school, college or other organisation, you can request that the centre completes the reference for you in the 'Apply' section of the UCAS website. For more information on the reference, please refer to the UCAS website.

ADMISSIONS TESTS AND WRITTEN WORK

For some universities, you may be asked to sit an Admissions Test (see Chapter 6). If you are applying for a course that requires you to sit an Admissions Test, you will need to register to sit the test.

For most tests, this registration must take place before 15th October. You will need to find an approved test centre to register with. You cannot register yourself, but must apply to a test centre, which is usually your school. If your school is not an approved test centre, you can find a list of approved centres worldwide on the Admissions Testing Service's website. Dates and costs for taking Admission Tests can also be found on the Admissions Testing Service's website.

THE INTERVIEW

As an international student, you may have different interview options available to you depending on your home country and the university you are applying to. Some universities have options available for applicants to be interviewed abroad or over Skype; more information can be found on the individual university websites. However, we recommend that, if possible, students have a face-to-face interview – in order to have the same experience and opportunity as other applicants.

SPECIAL INFORMATION FOR CAMBRIDGE APPLICANTS

Applicants considering applying to Cambridge need to be aware of specific aspects of their application process, including the Supplementary Application Questionnaire, the Cambridge Online Preliminary Application, and possible earlier deadlines for those wishing to be interviewed abroad. Full details of this can be found on the Cambridge website (www.cam.ac.uk).

VISAS

If you are offered a place at a UK university but you are not a national from the European Economic Area or Switzerland, you will need to apply for a Tier 4 student visa in your home country before you begin your studies.

The UK Border Agency requires you to be formally sponsored by a licensed UK higher education institution. The university will sponsor you, but only once your offer becomes unconditional. This means you must have gained a place and met all the academic and financial conditions before you can apply for a visa.

As circumstances for individuals vary, please visit the university websites in order to find out the full requirements. Visa details for interviews in the UK can be also found on the universities' websites.

QUOTAS FOR INTERNATIONAL MEDICINE APPLICANTS

As an international applicant, it is important to be aware of the high level of competition for places at UK medical schools. The number of international (non-EU) students that UK medical schools can take is limited to 7.5% of the total intake. Different medical schools have their own policies on how many places they offer, but some will not take any applicants from countries where a first degree in Medicine is offered, so it is best to check before applying.

For example:
- Oxford has 14 places for international (non-EU) Medicine applicants across both the standard and Graduate Entry courses each year.
- Cambridge has 22 places for international (non-EU) Medicine applicants for the undergraduate course.
- Sheffield and Glasgow each have 18 places for international (non-EU) Medicine applicants for the undergraduate course.
- UCL has 24 places for international (non-EU) Medicine applicants for the undergraduate course.
- Dundee has 11 places for international (non-EU) Medicine applicants for the undergraduate course.

If you are an international applicant interested in becoming a doctor, it is also worth considering applying for a different undergraduate course, such as Biomedical Sciences, Biochemistry, Biological Sciences or Biological Natural Sciences, before applying for a Graduate Medicine course.

10 LIFE AS A DOCTOR

Life as a Doctor

Your first shift will be a true test of your capabilities as a doctor. It will allow you to practically apply the skillset you have been cultivating over the course of your degree, and truly experience a taste of what the rest of your medical career holds.

Below are two first-hand accounts of what a shift as a doctor may look like.

MR WILLIAM LYNN

MBBS(Dist) BSc(Hons) FRCS (GenSurg) ChM

A day in the life of a surgical registrar

It's ten years ago that I did my first shift as a junior doctor and whilst my duties have expanded as my experience has increased, the job is a very different one compared to what it used to be. A series of cuts, loss of benefits and pension changes make a medical career different to what was on offer 17 years ago when I was accepted to medical school. I would urge anyone contemplating applying to medical school to keep this in mind!

My day starts at 6.15am to ensure I arrive into the hospital early to see the patients that I will be operating on. On today's list is a patient for removal of the gallbladder and two patients for complex weight loss surgery. As I'm quite senior I'll be doing the cases with the consultant watching me and helping where needed.

The first case is straight forward but the second is more challenging needing extra time than planned and high levels of concentration and precision. After the operation, without a break, I start to write operating notes and checking my emails. Outpatient scans have to be ordered and letters signed off. All this is achieved whilst eating lunch at the computer waiting for the next case to be anaesthetised. The complex afternoon case goes well but again takes a long time and by the end of it I'm shattered but very pleased with the results. I write another operation note, review the post-op patient that I've not managed to see in between cases and then today leave on time for once at 5pm. It has been a challenging and tiring day; however, it has also been extremely interesting and stimulating.

Long hours, missing spending time with your family and friends is part of being a doctor and the unpredictable nature of a career in surgery means that plans often have to be cancelled last minute. However, there are few more satisfying things than an operation performed well, with good patient outcomes. Going home at the end of the day knowing I have changed a person's life makes the early starts and busy days worthwhile. It's a long road to becoming a consultant but after 16 years of training, countless exams, large amounts of money spent on courses, memberships and travel to far flung parts of the world, I would do it all again without hesitation.

DR EMMA BRIERLEY
MB BChir MA(Hons) Cantab

My first shift
My first ever shift as a doctor was as a surgical house officer on a night shift in a busy teaching hospital. The SHO and registrar were called to theatre and I was left alone covering the wards. My bleep was going constantly and I had to remain calm, organised and prioritise.

I had a patient in A&E with abdominal pain who when I examined him had a suspected leaking aortic abdominal aneurysm, a vascular patient in severe pain with no lower leg pulses, a patient in day surgery who was due to go home but was tachycardic and multiple drug charts and fluid charts which needed medications prescribed.

This situation tested all the skills I had learnt and developed during my medical training.

The night was extremely stressful, tiring and demanding but I relished using the knowledge and experience I had developed over the past 6 years of hard work.

After experiencing many different specialties, I found my passion in palliative medicine. Spending time with a patient and their families during such a difficult period, helping them in numerous ways ranging from pain relief to listening to their fears provided me with immense job satisfaction.

My advice for prospective doctors is to undertake as much work experience as possible. Spending time shadowing and learning from a consultant is great but it is a long road before you achieve this status. Many years will be spent as a junior doctor and it is vital you experience how demanding this role is. This will give you an insight into medicine which is not only essential for applying for medical school but more importantly to confirm that medicine is definitely the career for you.

Our Other Titles

SO YOU WANT TO STUDY IN AMERICA? A GUIDE TO UNDERGRADUATE ADMISSIONS

For many students today, a place at a top US university is the ultimate academic aspiration. Institutions such as Harvard, Yale and Stanford, repeatedly sit high on the list of the world's best universities, as well as offering a world-class liberal arts education, and providing a foundation for an international career.

This book draws on decades of expertise in US university admissions to help you maximise your chance of success at one of these prestigious institutions. Our guide covers the entire journey of US college applications: from learning about the basics of the American system and choosing the college that bests fits your needs, to sitting the SATs, writing admissions essays and coordinating the various elements of each application.

Applying for top US universities is challenging, but success is possible with careful, well-informed planning. Throughout your application journey, we also provide guidance on the question of funding; how your parents and your school can help you succeed; and how to prepare for living in the US.

'This is an invaluable book for students (and their parents) trying to unravel the complexities of the US college application process and one which will definitely help you to decide if higher education in the US is right for you. Highly recommended.'

HILARY MARTIN, CAREERS & HIGHER EDUCATION ADVISER, BENENDEN SCHOOL

SO YOU WANT TO GO TO OXBRIDGE? TELL ME ABOUT A BANANA...

Applicants to Oxford and Cambridge are ambitious, academically-gifted, and accomplished – so how do Admissions Tutors decide who is offered that highly competitive place? And when an interviewer asks you to 'tell me about a banana', what exactly are they looking for in your answer?

So you want to go to Oxbridge? Tell me about a banana... is full of practical advice on how to make an informed application to Oxbridge at each stage of the increasingly competitive admissions process, featuring contributions from former Admissions Tutors and the team at Oxbridge Applications, the education consultancy.

This edition includes 50 new interview questions, and chapters on submitting written work, reapplying to Oxbridge, and the Oxbridge Admissions Tests. This guide draws on the experiences of thousands of successful Oxbridge graduates who provide insight into how they would approach the application process if they had to do it all over again.

'Tell me about a banana is an excellently clear and helpful survey of Oxbridge courses, colleges and application procedures – an invaluable guide for anyone considering an application to either great institution.'

GUY NOBES, MARLBOROUGH COLLEGE